Ninja Slushi

Recipe Book for Beginners

Transform Your Favorite Ingredients into Refreshing Slushies, Creamy Milkshakes, and Vibrant Frozen Treats with Effortless Recipes for Every Occasion

Karen Nicoletti

Table of Contents

01   **Introduction**

02   **Fundamentals of Ninja Slushi**

15   **Chapter 1 Classic Slushies**

34   **Chapter 2 Spiked Slush Slushies**

55   **Chapter 3 Frappe Slushies**

70   **Chapter 4 Milkshake Slushies**

85   **Chapter 5 Frozen Juice Slushies**

95   **Conclusion**

96   **Appendix 1 Measurement Conversion Chart**

97   **Appendix 2 Recipes Index**

Introduction

The Ninja Slushi Professional Frozen Drink Maker is the ultimate tool for creating indulgent frozen beverages right from the comfort of your home. Whether you're entertaining guests, cooling off on a hot summer day, or simply craving a treat, this versatile machine allows you to craft everything from refreshing slushies to creamy milkshakes with professional precision. Designed for convenience, the Ninja Slushi Professional takes the guesswork out of creating the perfect frozen drink, offering a user-friendly experience with customizable features to match any taste.

This innovative appliance features advanced RapidChill technology, which quickly transforms your favorite beverages into icy delights. Its multiple preset functions allow you to make a variety of drinks, including slushies, spiked slushies, frappés, milkshakes, and frozen juices. With easy-to-use controls, a high-performance motor, and effortless cleaning, the Ninja Slushi Professional is perfect for beginners and seasoned home drink makers alike.

To complement this incredible machine, the Ninja Slushi Recipe Book for Beginners serves as your ultimate guide to exploring the full potential of frozen drink creativity. Packed with an array of beginner-friendly recipes, this book offers step-by-step instructions to help you master everything from tangy fruit slushies to rich dessert drinks. Whether you're experimenting with fresh fruit blends, indulging in decadent frappés, or crafting kid-friendly mocktails, the recipe book inspires a world of frozen drink possibilities.

Transform your kitchen into a frozen beverage haven and impress your family and friends with creations that rival café-quality drinks. With the Ninja Slushi Professional Frozen Drink Maker and its accompanying recipe book, every sip becomes an experience to savor.

Fundamentals of Ninja Slushi

The Ninja Slushi Professional Frozen Drink Maker is a state-of-the-art appliance designed to create a variety of frozen beverages effortlessly. It uses advanced RapidChill technology to freeze and blend liquids into slushies, milkshakes, frappés, and more with precision and speed. The machine features multiple preset functions tailored to different drink types, ensuring the perfect texture and consistency for every creation.

Equipped with a high-performance motor and user-friendly controls, the Ninja Slushi offers both versatility and convenience. Its customizable settings allow you to adjust textures, catering to personal preferences for thickness or smoothness. Cleaning is a breeze with dishwasher-safe parts, making maintenance hassle-free. Whether for casual enjoyment or entertaining, the Ninja Slushi turns every drink into a refreshing treat.

What Is Ninja Slushi Professional Frozen Drink Maker?

The Ninja Slushi Professional Frozen Drink Maker is your go-to appliance for creating a wide range of frozen beverages with ease and precision. Designed to bring the joy of customized drinks to your home, this machine is perfect for making everything from slushies and milkshakes to frappés and frozen juices, ensuring a delicious treat for every occasion.

What sets the Ninja Slushi apart is its innovative RapidChill technology, which quickly transforms your favorite liquids into perfectly textured frozen drinks. With a selection of preset options, you can effortlessly prepare a variety of creations, including fruit-based slushies, spiked cocktails, and thick, creamy milkshakes. The machine even allows for texture adjustments, so you can tailor your drink to be as smooth or as icy as you like.

The appliance's intuitive design makes it simple to operate, whether you're an experienced home chef or a beginner. Just add your ingredients, select the appropriate setting, and let the Ninja Slushi work its magic. Its compact size and sleek design mean it fits seamlessly into any kitchen, while its easy-to-clean, dishwasher-safe components make post-drink cleanup a breeze.

Perfect for family gatherings, summer parties, or solo indulgence, the Ninja Slushi Professional Frozen Drink Maker is a versatile and fun addition to your kitchen. Experience the convenience of creating restaurant-quality frozen beverages from the comfort of your home and let your creativity shine with every drink!

Using the Control Panel

Power: Press to power the unit on and off.

Rinse Cycle: This cycle agitates, without cooling, to rinse the unit.

Presets: 5 unique presets use RapidChill Technology to determine the perfect temperature for the ideal frozen drink.

♠ **Slushi:** Creates perfectly textured slushies by blending ice and liquids with RapidChill Technology, delivering refreshing, finely crushed frozen drinks ideal for all ages and occasions.

♠ **Spiked Slushi:** Designed for adult beverages, it crafts smooth, alcohol-infused slushies by precisely chilling and blending drinks while maintaining an ideal balance of texture and flavor.

♠ **Frappé:** Produces creamy, café-style frappés by blending ice, milk, and flavoring into a silky consistency, perfect for recreating your favorite coffee shop drinks at home.

♠ **Milkshake:** Transforms ice cream, milk, and mix-ins into thick, decadent milkshakes with a velvety

finish, offering a nostalgic treat for any dessert lover.

♠ **Frozen Juice:** Turns juice into a smooth, icy beverage by rapidly freezing and churning, preserving the natural sweetness and creating a refreshing drink for hot days.

Temperature Control Setting:

♠ Each preset will start at a default/optimal temperature for ideal texture. If desired, adjust the temperature for your perfect frozen drink texture.

♠ For sippable frozen drinks, decrease the temperature level by pressing the bottom arrow on the control panel.

♠ For thicker, colder frozen drinks, increase the temperature level by pressing the top arrow on the control panel.

Benefits of Using It

The Ninja Slushi Professional Frozen Drink Maker is more than just a kitchen gadget—it's a game-changer for anyone who loves refreshing, frozen beverages. Here's why this innovative machine stands out and why it deserves a place in your home.

Customizable Creations

The Ninja Slushi allows you to tailor every drink to your preferences. From fruity slushies and creamy milkshakes to frozen juices and spiked cocktails, the machine's versatile presets let you craft the perfect drink for any occasion. Whether you like a smooth texture or a chunkier consistency, the Ninja Slushi offers adjustable settings to meet your needs.

RapidChill Technology

Thanks to its advanced RapidChill technology, the Ninja Slushi delivers frozen drinks quickly and efficiently. This means you can transform your favorite liquids—juice, soda, or even cocktails—into icy delights in just minutes. It's perfect for beating the heat or satisfying last-minute cravings.

Healthier Alternatives

The machine enables you to create healthier versions of your favorite frozen treats. Control the amount of sugar, fat, and additives in your drinks by using natural ingredients like fresh fruit, yogurt, and low-sugar options. Enjoy guilt-free indulgence while staying in control of your diet.

Convenience and Ease of Use

Operating the Ninja Slushi is simple, even for beginners. The intuitive control panel features clearly labeled presets, such as slush, frappé, and milkshake, making it easy to choose the right function. Plus, its dishwasher-safe components ensure quick and hassle-free cleaning.

Perfect for All Occasions

Whether you're hosting a summer barbecue, a holiday party, or a cozy movie night, the Ninja Slushi fits every event. Its ability to make multiple types of frozen beverages means there's something for everyone, from kids' slushies to adults' spiked drinks.

Cost-Effective

Save money by creating restaurant-quality frozen drinks at home. Instead of spending on expensive outings, you can use everyday ingredients to craft premium beverages tailored to your taste.

Compact and Stylish Design

Despite its powerful capabilities, the Ninja Slushi features a sleek and compact design that fits neatly into any kitchen. Its modern look enhances

your countertop without taking up too much space.

Durable and Reliable

Built with high-quality materials, the Ninja Slushi is designed for long-lasting use. It's a reliable investment for families, individuals, and party enthusiasts alike.

From convenience and creativity to health-conscious benefits, the Ninja Slushi Professional Frozen Drink Maker is the ultimate appliance for frozen drink lovers.

Before First Use

To ensure the best performance and longevity of your Ninja Slushi Professional Frozen Drink Maker, follow these steps before its first use:

1. Unpack and Inspect

Carefully remove the machine and all accessories from the packaging. Check for any visible damage or missing components. Remove all promotional stickers, tape, and labels.

2. Read the Manual

Familiarize yourself with the user manual, paying close attention to safety guidelines, operational instructions, and care tips. This will help you understand the functionality of the machine and avoid potential mishaps.

3. Clean Components

Wash all removable parts, including the vessel, evaporator, auger, and any included accessories, in warm, soapy water. Rinse thoroughly and allow them to air dry. Do not submerge the motor base or use a dishwasher for non-dishwasher-safe components.

4. Check Placement

Position the unit on a flat, sturdy surface with at least 6 inches of clearance around it for proper ventilation. Avoid placing it near heat sources or under low cabinets.

5. Run a Rinse Cycle

Before using the machine for the first time, perform a rinse cycle to clean the internal components. Fill the vessel with hot water to the max fill line and run the rinse function, then discard the water.

Now your Ninja Slushi is ready for its first frozen drink adventure!

Step-By-Step Using It

The Ninja Slushi Professional Frozen Drink Maker is designed to create delicious, frozen beverages with ease. Follow these steps to get the best results from your machine:

Preparation

Choose a Stable Surface: Place the unit on a clean, flat surface to ensure stability during use.

Clean Before Use: Make sure all parts are thoroughly cleaned and assembled as per the user manual. Attach the condensation catcher beneath the evaporator.

Chill Ingredients: Pre-chill liquids, as cold starting temperatures yield the best results. Do not use hot ingredients.

Step-by-Step Process

1. Add Ingredients

Open the top cover and pour your pre-chilled ingredients into the vessel.

Ensure the liquid meets the required sugar content (minimum 4%) or alcohol percentage (2.8%–16% for Spiked Slushies).

Do not exceed the maximum fill line (64 oz) for optimal performance.

2. Select Your Preset

Close the cover securely.

Turn on the unit by pressing the Power button.

Choose your desired preset (Slushi, Spiked Slushi, Frappé, Milkshake, or Frozen Juice) based on the type of beverage you're making.

3. Adjust Settings if Needed

Use the Temperature Control Arrows to modify the texture of your frozen drink. Increase the temperature for a smoother consistency or decrease it for a thicker texture.

Once ready, press the Start/Pause button to begin the chilling and churning process.

4. Monitor the Process

Watch the display to track the progress. The machine will automatically adjust and stop once the preset program is complete.

Serving Your Frozen Drink

1. Place a cup beneath the dispensing handle.
2. Slowly pull the handle forward to dispense your drink.
3. Release the handle to stop the flow and avoid spilling.

After Use

1. Turn off the machine by pressing the Power button.
2. Remove any remaining drink and clean all parts immediately. Use the Rinse cycle for quick cleaning before disassembly.

Enjoy the ease and versatility of the Ninja Slushi Professional Frozen Drink Maker for all your frozen beverage needs!

 ## Tips and Tricks for Using the Ninja Slushi

To get the most out of your Ninja Slushi Professional Frozen Drink Maker, follow these tips and tricks for optimal performance and delicious results:

Pre-Chill Ingredients

Always start with cold liquids to speed up the freezing process and achieve a smoother texture.
Refrigerate juices, dairy, or blended mixtures before adding them to the machine.

Maintain the Right Sugar Content

Ensure that your ingredients have a minimum sugar content of 4%. This is essential for proper freezing and a smooth consistency.
For healthier options, natural sweeteners like honey or agave syrup work well.

Use Alcohol Wisely

For Spiked Slushies, use beverages with an alcohol content between 2.8% and 16%. Too much alcohol can prevent proper freezing.
Mix alcoholic drinks with a non-alcoholic base to balance consistency.

Experiment with Temperature Control

Adjust the temperature settings to customize your drink's texture. Lower the temperature for thicker slushies and higher for smoother, more sippable drinks.
Start with the default preset and tweak as needed for your preferences.

Avoid Hot Ingredients

Never add hot liquids, as they can damage the machine or significantly delay the freezing process.

Secure Lightweight Ingredients

For drinks that include lightweight toppings, like whipped cream or sliced fruits, secure them with a stir stick to prevent splattering during dispensing.

Use the Rinse Cycle After Each Use

The Rinse cycle is a quick and efficient way to clean the unit between drinks. This ensures no flavors mix and keeps the machine running smoothly.

Serve Immediately

Frozen drinks taste best fresh. Serve them immediately after dispensing for maximum flavor and consistency.

By following these tips, you'll maximize your Ninja Slushi experience, ensuring perfectly frozen beverages every time!

Clean and Maintenance of the Ninja Slushi

Proper cleaning and maintenance of your Ninja Slushi Professional Frozen Drink Maker will ensure it functions optimally and lasts for years. Follow these steps to keep your machine in pristine condition:

Daily Cleaning Routine

1. **Unplug the Machine:** Always unplug the unit before starting the cleaning process to ensure safety.

2. **Rinse Cycle:** Use the built-in rinse cycle after each use. Fill the vessel with warm water up to the max fill line and run the cycle. Dispense the water completely to remove any residual flavors or particles.

3. **Disassemble Components:** Remove the vessel, auger, and crisper plates from the machine. Carefully detach the spout and drip tray if applicable.

4. **Hand Wash Components:** Wash all removable parts with warm, soapy water. Avoid using abrasive sponges to prevent scratches. Rinse thoroughly and air-dry.

5. **Dishwasher Safety:** While some parts may be dishwasher safe, such as the vessel and crisper plates, avoid using heated drying cycles to prolong their lifespan.

6. **Clean the Evaporator:** Wipe the evaporator gently with a damp, sanitized cloth to remove any residue. Ensure it is completely dry before reassembling.

Weekly Deep Cleaning

Inspect and Clean the Condensation Catcher: Remove and empty the condensation catcher. Wash it thoroughly to prevent build-up.

Sanitize the Spout and Drip Tray: These areas can accumulate sticky residues. Clean them weekly using a mild cleaning solution and warm water.

General Maintenance Tips

1. **Keep the Motor Base Dry:** Wipe the motor base with a damp cloth but avoid soaking it. Never submerge the

base in water or place it in the dishwasher.

2. Store in a Dry Place: When not in use, store the machine in a cool, dry area to prevent moisture damage.

3. Check for Wear: Regularly inspect seals, gaskets, and other components for signs of wear and replace as needed to maintain functionality.

By following these cleaning and maintenance steps, your Ninja Slushi will stay in excellent condition, delivering perfectly frozen drinks for years to come.

Frequently Asked Questions and Notes

1. Can I use hot liquids in the Ninja Slushi?

No, do not add hot ingredients to the unit. Only use cold or room-temperature liquids to prevent damage to the internal components.

2. What types of ingredients work best for slushies?

Use liquids containing at least 4% sugar, such as juices, sodas, or sweetened beverages. This helps achieve the desired slushy texture. Sugar-free liquids may not produce optimal results.

3. Can I use alcohol for spiked slushies?

Yes, the Spiked Slushi preset is designed for beverages with an alcohol content between 2.8% and 16%. Be sure to measure carefully for the best results.

4. Are all parts dishwasher-safe?

Yes, most removable parts like the vessel, auger, and drip tray are dishwasher-safe. However, avoid using heated drying cycles to extend their lifespan.

5. What should I do if my drink isn't freezing properly?

Ensure your ingredients meet the required sugar content. Additionally, use chilled liquids and pre-frozen fruits for better results. If needed, increase the temperature setting for thicker textures.

6. Can I make dairy-free or vegan frozen drinks with the Ninja Slushi?

Absolutely! The Ninja Slushi works well with dairy-free milk alternatives such as almond milk, oat milk, or coconut milk. Just ensure the liquids meet the required sugar content for optimal freezing.

7. How long does it take to make a frozen drink?

Depending on the preset and ingredients, it typically takes 15–30 minutes to create a perfectly frozen drink. The duration may vary based on ingredient temperature and volume.

8. What is the minimum and maximum liquid capacity for the Ninja Slushi?

The unit requires a minimum of 16 ounces (2 cups) of liquid to operate properly, and the maximum capacity is 64 ounces (8 cups) to prevent overflows and ensure consistent results.

Notes

Ingredient Ratios: For consistent results, always follow the recommended ratios for liquids and solids. Overloading the unit may affect freezing performance.

Avoid Solid Ingredients: Do not add ice cubes, hard fruit, or other solid ingredients that could damage the auger or evaporator. Use pre-blended or soft components instead.

Temperature Adjustment: Adjust the temperature setting to customize drink texture. Decrease for smoother, more sippable drinks and increase for thicker, spoonable textures.

Regular Maintenance: Clean the unit thoroughly after each use. Ensure all components are dry before reassembling to maintain performance and hygiene.

Storage Tip: Store the unit upright in a cool, dry location to protect the internal mechanics and prevent damage.

These FAQs and notes will help you get the most out of your Ninja Slushi Professional Frozen Drink Maker while ensuring optimal performance and longevity.

Chapter 1 Classic Slushies

16   Mixed Berries Slushi
16   Coconut Pineapple Slushi
17   Peach and Basil Slushi
17   Lemonade Cherry Slushi
18   Cinnamon Chocolate Slushi
18   Cucumber & Honeydew Melon Slushi
19   Refreshing Peach, Apricot, and Orange Slushi
19   Mint Honeydew Slushi
20   Coconut Pineapple Slushi
20   Minty Berries Slushi
21   Homemade Citrus Blend Slushi
21   Tasty Cherry Cola Slushi
22   Mango Cantaloupe Slushi
22   Cherry Pomegranate Slushi
23   Grape and Blueberry Slushi
23   Flavorful Pineapple Orange Slushi
24   Strawberry Kiwi Slushi
24   Peach Mango Slushi

25   Rich Grape Slushi
25   Lime Watermelon Slushi
26   Berries Banana Slushi
26   Basic Mango Slushi
27   Fresh Grape Lemonade Slushi
27   Mint Orange Slushi
28   Fresh Raspberry Lemonade Slushi
28   Raspberry Slushi
29   Ginger Pineapple Slushi
29   Tropical Twist Slushi
30   Vanilla Root Beer Slushi
30   Refreshing Watermelon Strawberry Slushi
31   Mango Slushi
31   Ginger Peach Slushi
32   Flavorful Matcha Tea Slushi
32   Lemon Lime Sprite Slushi
33   Lime Cucumber Slushi
33   Peach Tea Slushi

Mixed Berries Slushi

Servings: 4

Ingredients:

1½ cups strawberries

1 cup blackberries

1 cup blueberries

¼ cup sugar (optional)

2 cups water

Preparation:

1. Place all the ingredients into a blender and blend until the mixture is smooth.

2. Pour the mixture into the Ninja Slushi vessel.

3. Select "SLUSH." The preset will start at the default/optimal temperature, which is excellent for the best texture.

4. If you'd like, you can modify the temperature to your preference.

5. When the frozen drink attains the desired temperature, the machine will beep three times.

6. Dispense and enjoy.

Coconut Pineapple Slushi

Servings: 2

Ingredients:

2 cups coconut water

1 cup pineapple

1 teaspoon pure vanilla extract

2 tablespoons sugar

Preparation:

1. Add all the ingredients to a blender and blend until smooth.

2. Pour the mixture into the Ninja Slushi vessel.

3. Select "SLUSH." The preset will start at the default/optimal temperature, which is excellent for the best texture.

4. If you'd like, you can modify the temperature to your preference.

5. When the frozen drink attains the desired temperature, the machine will beep three times.

6. Dispense and enjoy.

Peach and Basil Slushi

Servings: 4

Ingredients:

3 cups peach

3 cups water

6 fresh basil leaves, use hands to lightly

bend to release aroma

2 tablespoons of fresh lime juice

3 tablespoons sugar

Preparation:

1. Place all the ingredients into a blender and blend until the mixture is smooth.

2. Pour the mixture into the Ninja Slushi vessel.

3. Select "SLUSH." The preset will start at the default/optimal temperature, which is excellent for the best texture.

4. If you'd like, you can modify the temperature to your preference.

5. When the frozen drink attains the desired temperature, the machine will beep three times.

6. Dispense and enjoy.

Lemonade Cherry Slushi

Servings: 4

Ingredients:

3 cups cherries, pitted

¼ cup sugar

3 cups lemonade concentrate

A pinch of salt

½ cup lime juice

Preparation:

1. Place all the ingredients into a blender and blend until the mixture is smooth.

2. Pour the mixture into the Ninja Slushi vessel.

3. Select "SLUSH." The preset will start at the default/optimal temperature, which is excellent for the best texture.

4. If you'd like, you can modify the temperature to your preference.

5. When the frozen drink attains the desired temperature, the machine will beep three times.

6. Dispense and enjoy.

Cinnamon Chocolate Slushi

Servings: 4

Ingredients:

½ cup cocoa powder

1 teaspoon cinnamon

3 to 4 cups milk of your choice

1 teaspoon vanilla extract

¼ cup sugar

Preparation:

1. Combine all ingredients in a large pitcher and whisk until the sugar is fully dissolved.
2. Pour the mixture into the Ninja Slushi vessel.
3. Select "SLUSH." The preset will start at the default/optimal temperature, which is excellent for the best texture.
4. If you'd like, you can modify the temperature to your preference.
5. When the frozen drink attains the desired temperature, the machine will beep three times.
6. Dispense and enjoy.

Cucumber & Honeydew Melon Slushi

Servings: 2

Ingredients:

½ cucumber, peeled and chopped

2 cups water

2 tablespoons sugar

1 cup honeydew melon, diced

Preparation:

1. Place all the ingredients into a blender and blend until the mixture is smooth.
2. Pour the mixture into the Ninja Slushi vessel.
3. Select "SLUSH." The preset will start at the default/optimal temperature, which is excellent for the best texture.
4. If you'd like, you can modify the temperature to your preference.
5. When the frozen drink attains the desired temperature, the machine will beep three times.
6. Dispense and enjoy.

Refreshing Peach, Apricot, and Orange Slushi

Servings: 3-4

Ingredients:

1 tablespoon fresh mint leaves

2 cups apricot, slices/chunks

2 cups orange juice

¼ cup sugar

1 cup peach slices

½ cup fresh lime juice

Preparation:

1. Place all the ingredients into a blender and blend until the mixture is smooth.

2. Pour the mixture into the Ninja Slushi vessel.

3. Select "SLUSH." The preset will start at the default/optimal temperature, which is excellent for the best texture.

4. If you'd like, you can modify the temperature to your preference.

5. When the frozen drink attains the desired temperature, the machine will beep three times.

6. Dispense and enjoy.

Mint Honeydew Slushi

Servings: 4

Ingredients:

4 cups honeydew melon, chopped

3 cups water

¼ cup fresh mint leaves

¼ cup sugar

Preparation:

1. Place all the ingredients into a blender and blend until the mixture is smooth and the sugar is fully dissolved.

2. Pour the mixture into the Ninja Slushi vessel.

3. Select "SLUSH." The preset will start at the default/optimal temperature, which is excellent for the best texture.

4. If you'd like, you can modify the temperature to your preference.

5. When the frozen drink attains the desired temperature, the machine will beep three times.

6. Dispense and enjoy.

Coconut Pineapple Slushi

Servings: 2

Ingredients:

2 cups coconut water

½ cup coconut milk

2 tablespoons sugar

½ cup pineapple juice

Preparation:

1. Combine all ingredients in a large pitcher and whisk until the sugar is fully dissolved.
2. Pour the mixture into the Ninja Slushi vessel.
3. Select "SLUSH." The preset will start at the default/optimal temperature, which is excellent for the best texture.
4. If you'd like, you can modify the temperature to your preference.
5. When the frozen drink attains the desired temperature, the machine will beep three times.
6. Dispense and enjoy.

Minty Berries Slushi

Servings: 4

Ingredients:

1 cup of blueberries

1 cup of raspberries

¼ cup mint leaves

1 cup blueberries

2 to 3 cups water

1½ cups of strawberries

Sugar to taste, optional

Preparation:

1. Place all the ingredients into a blender and blend until the mixture is smooth.
2. Pour the mixture into the Ninja Slushi vessel.
3. Select "SLUSH." The preset will start at the default/optimal temperature, which is excellent for the best texture.
4. If you'd like, you can modify the temperature to your preference.
5. When the frozen drink attains the desired temperature, the machine will beep three times.
6. Dispense and enjoy.

Homemade Citrus Blend Slushi

Servings: 4

Ingredients:

2 cups lemonade concentrate

¼ cup fresh lime juice

2 cups orange juice

Sugar, to taste

Preparation:

1. Combine all ingredients in a large pitcher and whisk until the sugar is fully dissolved.
2. Pour the mixture into the Ninja Slushi vessel.
3. Select "SLUSH." The preset will start at the default/optimal temperature, which is excellent for the best texture.
4. If you'd like, you can modify the temperature to your preference.
5. When the frozen drink attains the desired temperature, the machine will beep three times.
6. Dispense and enjoy.

Tasty Cherry Cola Slushi

Servings: 3-4

Ingredients:

1½ cups cherry cola (regular)

1 tablespoon lime juice

½ cup cherry juice

Sugar, to taste

Preparation:

1. Combine the cherry cola, cherry juice, sugar, and lime juice in a large pitcher and whisk until the sugar is fully dissolved.
2. Pour the mixture into the Ninja Slushi vessel.
3. Select "SLUSH." The preset will start at the default/optimal temperature, which is excellent for the best texture.
4. If you'd like, you can modify the temperature to your preference.
5. When the frozen drink attains the desired temperature, the machine will beep three times.
6. Dispense and enjoy.

Mango Cantaloupe Slushi

Servings: 4

Ingredients:

2 cups mango

2 cups cantaloupe

2 to 3 cups water

1 teaspoon vanilla, optional

Sugar, to taste

Preparation:

1. Place all the ingredients into a blender and blend until the mixture is smooth.
2. Pour the mixture into the Ninja Slushi vessel.
3. Select "SLUSH." The preset will start at the default/optimal temperature, which is excellent for the best texture.
4. If you'd like, you can modify the temperature to your preference.
5. When the frozen drink attains the desired temperature, the machine will beep three times.
6. Dispense and enjoy.

Cherry Pomegranate Slushi

Servings: 4

Ingredients:

2 cups of cherries, pitted

1 tablespoon fresh lime juice

2 cups pomegranate juice

Sugar to taste, if needed

Preparation:

1. Place all the ingredients into a blender and blend until the mixture is smooth.
2. Pour the mixture into the Ninja Slushi vessel.
3. Select "SLUSH." The preset will start at the default/optimal temperature, which is excellent for the best texture.
4. If you'd like, you can modify the temperature to your preference.
5. When the frozen drink attains the desired temperature, the machine will beep three times.
6. Dispense and enjoy.

Grape and Blueberry Slushi

Servings: 4

Ingredients:

2 cups red grapes, seedless

2 cups blueberries

2 cups concord grape juice

3 to 4 tablespoons sugar, if needed

Preparation:

1. Place all the ingredients into a blender and blend until the mixture is smooth.
2. Pour the mixture into the Ninja Slushi vessel.
3. Select "SLUSH." The preset will start at the default/optimal temperature, which is excellent for the best texture.
4. If you'd like, you can modify the temperature to your preference.
5. When the frozen drink attains the desired temperature, the machine will beep three times.
6. Dispense and enjoy.

Flavorful Pineapple Orange Slushi

Servings: 4

Ingredients:

3 cups pineapple chunks

Sugar, to taste

2 cups orange juice

Preparation:

1. Place all the ingredients into a blender and blend until the mixture is smooth.
2. Pour the mixture into the Ninja Slushi vessel.
3. Select "SLUSH." The preset will start at the default/optimal temperature, which is excellent for the best texture.
4. If you'd like, you can modify the temperature to your preference.
5. When the frozen drink attains the desired temperature, the machine will beep three times.
6. Dispense and enjoy.

Strawberry Kiwi Slushi

Servings: 4

Ingredients:

2 cups strawberries

2 cups water

4 medium kiwis, peeled and sliced

¼ cup sugar

Preparation:

1. Place all the ingredients into a blender and blend until the mixture is smooth.
2. Pour the mixture into the Ninja Slushi vessel.
3. Select "SLUSH." The preset will start at the default/optimal temperature, which is excellent for the best texture.
4. If you'd like, you can modify the temperature to your preference.
5. When the frozen drink attains the desired temperature, the machine will beep three times.
6. Dispense and enjoy.

Peach Mango Slushi

Servings: 4

Ingredients:

3 cups peach, chunks

2 cups water

2 cups mango, chunks

¼ cup sugar

Preparation:

1. Place all the ingredients into a blender and blend until the mixture is smooth.
2. Pour the mixture into the Ninja Slushi vessel.
3. Select "SLUSH." The preset will start at the default/optimal temperature, which is excellent for the best texture.
4. If you'd like, you can modify the temperature to your preference.
5. When the frozen drink attains the desired temperature, the machine will beep three times.
6. Dispense and enjoy.

Rich Grape Slushi

Servings: 2-3

Ingredients:

2 cups grape juice

2 tablespoons sugar

¼ cup lemon juice

Preparation:

1. Mix grape juice, lemon juice, and sugar in a large pitcher and whisk until the sugar is fully dissolved.
2. Pour the mixture into the Ninja Slushi vessel.
3. Select "SLUSH." The preset will start at the default/optimal temperature, which is excellent for the best texture.
4. If you'd like, you can modify the temperature to your preference.
5. When the frozen drink attains the desired temperature, the machine will beep three times.
6. Dispense and enjoy.

Lime Watermelon Slushi

Servings: 4

Ingredients:

3 cups of watermelon, cubed

2 cups water

Sugar, to taste

¼ cup of fresh lime juice

Preparation:

1. Place all the ingredients into a blender and blend until the mixture is smooth.
2. Pour the mixture into the Ninja Slushi vessel.
3. Select "SLUSH." The preset will start at the default/optimal temperature, which is excellent for the best texture.
4. If you'd like, you can modify the temperature to your preference.
5. When the frozen drink attains the desired temperature, the machine will beep three times.
6. Dispense and enjoy.

Berries Banana Slushi

Servings: 2-4

Ingredients:

1 teaspoon fresh lemon juice

¼ cup Blueberries

1.5 cups strawberries

12 oz. Seltzer Water

1 medium size banana

1 tablespoon sugar

1 cup pitted cherries

Preparation:

1. Combine all of the ingredients in a blender and blend until smooth.

2. Pour the mixture into the Ninja Slushi vessel.

3. Select "SLUSH." The preset will start at the default/optimal temperature, which is excellent for the best texture.

4. If you prefer, you can adjust the temperature.

5. When the frozen drink attains the desired temperature, the machine will beep three times.

6. Serve immediately and enjoy.

Basic Mango Slushi

Servings: 2

Ingredients:

1¼ tablespoons sugar

2 fresh mangoes

1 cup water

Preparation:

1. Combine all of the ingredients in a blender and blend until smooth.

2. Pour the mixture into the Ninja Slushi vessel.

3. Select "SLUSH." The preset will start at the default/optimal temperature, which is excellent for the best texture.

4. If you prefer, you can adjust the temperature.

5. When the frozen drink attains the desired temperature, the machine will beep three times.

6. Serve immediately and enjoy.

Fresh Grape Lemonade Slushi

Servings: 2-4

Ingredients:

4 cups seedless grapes (red or green)

2 tablespoons sugar

3 teaspoons lemon juice

1 cup water

Preparation:

1. Combine all of the ingredients in a blender and blend until smooth.
2. Pour the mixture into the Ninja Slushi vessel.
3. Select "SLUSH." The preset will start at the default/optimal temperature, which is excellent for the best texture.
4. If you prefer, you can adjust the temperature.
5. When the frozen drink attains the desired temperature, the machine will beep three times.
6. Serve immediately and enjoy.

Mint Orange Slushi

Servings: 2

Ingredients:

1 cup fresh orange juice

1½ cups water

2-3 tablespoons sugar

1 teaspoon orange powder, optional

¼ cup fresh mint leaves

Preparation:

1. Combine all of the ingredients in a blender and blend until smooth.
2. Pour the mixture into the Ninja Slushi vessel.
3. Select "SLUSH." The preset will start at the default/optimal temperature, which is excellent for the best texture.
4. If you prefer, you can adjust the temperature.
5. When the frozen drink attains the desired temperature, the machine will beep three times.
6. Serve immediately and enjoy.

Fresh Raspberry Lemonade Slushi

Servings: 2

Ingredients:

½ cup fresh raspberries

2 cups lemonade

2 tablespoons sugar

Preparation:

1. Combine all of the ingredients in a blender and blend until smooth.
2. Pour the mixture into the Ninja Slushi vessel.
3. Select "SLUSH." The preset will start at the default/optimal temperature, which is excellent for the best texture.
4. If you prefer, you can adjust the temperature.
5. When the frozen drink attains the desired temperature, the machine will beep three times.
6. Serve immediately and enjoy.

Raspberry Slushi

Servings: 2-4

Ingredients:

1½ cups frozen raspberries

1 cup water

½ cup sugar

1 tablespoon lemon juice

Preparation:

1. Combine all of the ingredients in a blender and blend until smooth.
2. Pour the mixture into the Ninja Slushi vessel.
3. Select "SLUSH." The preset will start at the default/optimal temperature, which is excellent for the best texture.
4. If you prefer, you can adjust the temperature.
5. When the frozen drink attains the desired temperature, the machine will beep three times.
6. Serve immediately and enjoy.

Ginger Pineapple Slushi

Servings: 2

Ingredients:

2 cups pineapple juice

1 teaspoon fresh grated ginger

1 tablespoon sugar

Preparation:

1. Combine all of the ingredients in a blender and blend until smooth.
2. Pour the mixture into the Ninja Slushi vessel.
3. Select "SLUSH." The preset will start at the default/optimal temperature, which is excellent for the best texture.
4. If you prefer, you can adjust the temperature.
5. When the frozen drink attains the desired temperature, the machine will beep three times.
6. Serve immediately and enjoy.

Tropical Twist Slushi

Servings: 3-4

Ingredients:

1 cup fresh pineapple chunks

1 cup peach nectar

½ cup mango nectar

2 tablespoons sugar

½ cup coconut water

Preparation:

1. Combine all of the ingredients in a blender and blend until smooth.
2. Pour the mixture into the Ninja Slushi vessel.
3. Select "SLUSH." The preset will start at the default/optimal temperature, which is excellent for the best texture.
4. If you prefer, you can adjust the temperature.
5. When the frozen drink attains the desired temperature, the machine will beep three times.
6. Serve immediately and enjoy.

Vanilla Root Beer Slushi

Servings: 2

Ingredients:

1 (16 ounce) bottle root beer

¼ teaspoon vanilla extract

3 tablespoons heavy cream

1½ cups root beer, regular

1 tablespoon sugar

Preparation:

1. Combine all ingredients in a large pitcher and whisk until the sugar is fully dissolved.

2. Pour the mixture into the Ninja Slushi vessel.

3. Select "SLUSH." The preset will start at the default/optimal temperature, which is excellent for the best texture.

4. If you prefer, you can adjust the temperature.

5. When the frozen drink attains the desired temperature, the machine will beep three times.

6. Serve immediately and enjoy.

Refreshing Watermelon Strawberry Slushi

Servings: 2-4

Ingredients:

⅓ cup lemon juice

1 cup water

2 cups cubed seedless watermelon

⅓ cup sugar

2 cups fresh strawberries

Preparation:

1. Combine all of the ingredients in a blender and blend until smooth.

2. Pour the mixture into the Ninja Slushi vessel.

3. Select "SLUSH." The preset will start at the default/optimal temperature, which is excellent for the best texture.

4. If you prefer, you can adjust the temperature.

5. When the frozen drink attains the desired temperature, the machine will beep three times.

6. Serve immediately and enjoy.

Mango Slushi

Servings: 2-3

Ingredients:

2 cups mango juice

1 tablespoon sugar

2 tablespoons lime juice

Preparation:

1. Combine all of the ingredients in a blender and blend until smooth.
2. Pour the mixture into the Ninja Slushi vessel.
3. Select "SLUSH." The preset will start at the default/optimal temperature, which is excellent for the best texture.
4. If you prefer, you can adjust the temperature.
5. When the frozen drink attains the desired temperature, the machine will beep three times.
6. Serve immediately and enjoy.

Ginger Peach Slushi

Servings: 2-3

Ingredients:

1 tablespoon fresh ginger, finely grated

2 ripe peaches, peeled and chopped

1½ cups water

¼ cup sugar

Preparation:

1. Combine all of the ingredients in a blender and blend until smooth.
2. Pour the mixture into the Ninja Slushi vessel.
3. Select "SLUSH." The preset will start at the default/optimal temperature, which is excellent for the best texture.
4. If you prefer, you can adjust the temperature.
5. When the frozen drink attains the desired temperature, the machine will beep three times.
6. Serve immediately and enjoy.

Flavorful Matcha Tea Slushi

Servings: 2

Ingredients:

2 tablespoons matcha tea powder   ⅓ cup sugar

2 cups water

Preparation:

1. Combine all ingredients in a large pitcher and whisk until the sugar is fully dissolved.

2. Pour the mixture into the Ninja Slushi vessel.

3. Select "SLUSH." The preset will start at the default/optimal temperature, which is excellent for the best texture.

4. If you prefer, you can adjust the temperature.

5. When the frozen drink attains the desired temperature, the machine will beep three times.

6. Serve immediately and enjoy.

Lemon Lime Sprite Slushi

Servings: 4

Ingredients:

¾ cup granulated sugar   4 fresh limes- peeled

1 cup water   2 teaspoons lemon zest

2 fresh lemons- peeled   1 Liter of Sprite

Preparation:

1. Cut off the lemon and lime peels. Place the lemons and limes in a blender and then blend. If you don't like pulp, strain it out at this stage.

2. Now, combine all the other ingredients in a blender and blend until smooth.

3. Pour the mixture into the Ninja Slushi vessel.

4. Select "SLUSH." The preset will start at the default/optimal temperature, which is excellent for the best texture.

5. If you prefer, you can adjust the temperature.

6. When the frozen drink attains the desired temperature, the machine will beep three times.

7. Serve immediately and enjoy.

Lime Cucumber Slushi

Servings: 2

Ingredients:

2 cups cucumber juice

2 tablespoons sugar

2 tablespoons lime juice

Preparation:

1. Combine all ingredients in a large pitcher and whisk until the sugar is fully dissolved.
2. Pour the mixture into the Ninja Slushi vessel.
3. Select "SLUSH." The preset will start at the default/optimal temperature, which is excellent for the best texture.
4. If you prefer, you can adjust the temperature.
5. When the frozen drink attains the desired temperature, the machine will beep three times.
6. Serve immediately and enjoy.

Peach Tea Slushi

Servings: 2

Ingredients:

1 cup water

2-3 fresh sliced peaches

1 cup sugar

3 tea bags (green, or black)

6 cups water

Preparation:

1. In a saucepan, heat 6 cups of water to a boil. Turn off the flame and allow to cool for about 5 minutes. Then, put the tea bags and brew for 5–6 minutes.
2. Remove the tea bags. Avoid squeezing the tea bag since this can release tannins that make the tea bitter.
3. Combine all of the ingredients in a blender and blend until smooth.
4. Pour the mixture into the Ninja Slushi vessel.
5. Select "SLUSH." The preset will start at the default/optimal temperature, which is excellent for the best texture.
6. If you prefer, you can adjust the temperature.
7. When the frozen drink attains the desired temperature, the machine will beep three times.
8. Serve immediately and enjoy.

Chapter 2 Spiked Slush Slushies

35   Pineapple Rum Slushi

35   Homemade Champagne Cocktail Slushi

36   Classic Margarita Slushi

36   Moscato Pomegranate Slushi

37   Strawberry Rum Slushi

37   Honeydew Rum Slushi

38   Lime Margaritas Slushi

38   Sweet Lemonade Slushi

39   Lemon Strawberry Vodka Slushi

39   Passion Fruit Rum Slushi

40   Citrus White Wine Slushi

40   Spiked Pina Rum Slushi

41   Delicious Pomegranate Gin Slushi

41   Paloma Spiked Slushi

42   Classic Bloody Mary Slushi

42   Aromatic Martini Slushi

43   Raspberry Peach Slushi

43   Refreshing Mojito Slushi

44   Sparkling Berries Slushi

44   Orange Tequila Slushi

45   Sangria Red Wine Slushi

45   Lemon Strawberry Daiquiri Slushi

46   Flavorful Margarita Cocktail Slushi

46   Delicious Mudslide Slushi

47   Lime Grapefruit Paloma Slushi

47   Mint Blackberry Bourbon Slushi

48   Classic Peach Bellini Slushi

48   Vanilla Eggnog Bourbon Slushi

49   Lemonade Spiked Slushi

49   Refreshing Blue Lagoon Slushi

50   Mint Watermelon Tequila Slushi

50   Tasty Mai Tai Slushi

51   Tropical Rum Slushi

51   Lemon Cucumber Gin Slushi

52   Lime Cranberry Vodka Slushi

52   Pineapple Colada Slushi

53   Passion Fruit Cocktail Slushi

53   Lime Gin and Tonic Slushi

54   Sparkling Peach White Wine Slushi

Pineapple Rum Slushi

Servings: 8

Ingredients:

¼ cup Key lime juice

3½ cups unsweetened pineapple juice

1 cup coconut rum

3 tablespoons grenadine syrup or Campari liqueur

1½ cups orange juice

1 cup orange peach mango juice

1 cup coconut water

1 cup dark rum

Preparation:

1. In a large pitcher, combine the first 8 ingredients and whisk until everything is fully mixed.
2. Pour the mixture into the Ninja Slushi vessel.
3. Select "SPIKED SLUSH." The preset will start at the default/optimal temperature, which is excellent for the best texture.
4. If you'd like, you can modify the temperature to your preference.
5. When the frozen drink attains the desired temperature, the machine will beep three times.
6. Dispense and enjoy.

Homemade Champagne Cocktail Slushi

Servings: 1-2

Ingredients:

½ teaspoon sugar

½-ounce brandy

½ cup champagne

6 dashes bitters

Preparation:

1. Combine all ingredients in a large pitcher and whisk until the sugar is fully dissolved.
2. Pour the mixture into the Ninja Slushi vessel.
3. Select "SPIKED SLUSH." The preset will start at the default/optimal temperature, which is excellent for the best texture.
4. If you'd like, you can modify the temperature to your preference.
5. When the frozen drink attains the desired temperature, the machine will beep three times.
6. Dispense and enjoy.

Classic Margarita Slushi

Servings: 2-3

Ingredients:

½ cup triple sec

½ cup tequila

1 cup lime juice

Preparation:

1. Add lime juice, tequila, triple sec, and ice in a large pitcher and whisk until everything is fully mixed.
2. Pour the mixture into the Ninja Slushi vessel.
3. Select "SPIKED SLUSH." The preset will start at the default/optimal temperature, which is excellent for the best texture.
4. If you'd like, you can modify the temperature to your preference.
5. When the frozen drink attains the desired temperature, the machine will beep three times.
6. Dispense and enjoy.

Moscato Pomegranate Slushi

Servings: 4

Ingredients:

3 cups pomegranate juice

1 cup Moscato

Sugar to taste, if needed

Preparation:

1. Combine all ingredients in a large pitcher and whisk until the sugar is fully dissolved.
2. Pour the mixture into the Ninja Slushi vessel.
3. Select "SPIKED SLUSH." The preset will start at the default/optimal temperature, which is excellent for the best texture.
4. If you'd like, you can modify the temperature to your preference.
5. When the frozen drink attains the desired temperature, the machine will beep three times.
6. Dispense and enjoy.

Strawberry Rum Slushi

Servings: 2-3

Ingredients:

1½ cups fresh strawberries

½ cup lime juice

½ cup rum

Sugar, to taste

Preparation:

1. Place all the ingredients into a blender and blend until the mixture is smooth.
2. Pour the mixture into the Ninja Slushi vessel.
3. Select "SPIKED SLUSH." The preset will start at the default/optimal temperature, which is excellent for the best texture.
4. If you'd like, you can modify the temperature to your preference.
5. When the frozen drink attains the desired temperature, the machine will beep three times.
6. Dispense and enjoy.

Honeydew Rum Slushi

Servings: 4

Ingredients:

¼ cup rum

3 cups honeydew melon, chopped

¼ cup sugar

¼ cup lemon juice

Preparation:

1. Place all the ingredients into a blender and blend until the mixture is smooth.
2. Pour the mixture into the Ninja Slushi vessel.
3. Select "SPIKED SLUSH." The preset will start at the default/optimal temperature, which is excellent for the best texture.
4. If you'd like, you can modify the temperature to your preference.
5. When the frozen drink attains the desired temperature, the machine will beep three times.
6. Dispense and enjoy.

Lime Margaritas Slushi

Servings: 4

Ingredients:

½ cup tequila

2 tablespoons superfine sugar

¼ cup triple sec

¼ cup lemon juice

¼ cup lime juice

1 tablespoon kosher salt

Preparation:

1. Combine all ingredients in a large pitcher and whisk until the sugar is fully dissolved.
2. Pour the mixture into the Ninja Slushi vessel.
3. Select "SPIKED SLUSH." The preset will start at the default/optimal temperature, which is excellent for the best texture.
4. If you'd like, you can modify the temperature to your preference.
5. When the frozen drink attains the desired temperature, the machine will beep three times.
6. Dispense and enjoy.

Sweet Lemonade Slushi

Servings: 8

Ingredients:

2¼ cups sugar

1 cup light rum or vodka

1 tablespoon grated lemon zest

5 cups water, divided

1¾ cups lemon juice

Preparation:

1. Combine all ingredients in a large pitcher and whisk until the sugar is fully dissolved.
2. Pour the mixture into the Ninja Slushi vessel.
3. Select "SPIKED SLUSH." The preset will start at the default/optimal temperature, which is excellent for the best texture.
4. If you'd like, you can modify the temperature to your preference.
5. When the frozen drink attains the desired temperature, the machine will beep three times.
6. Dispense and enjoy.

Lemon Strawberry Vodka Slushi

Servings: 4

Ingredients:

3 cups strawberries

¼ cup vodka

1 cup fresh lemon juice

Sugar to taste, optional

Preparation:

1. Place all the ingredients into a blender and blend until the mixture is smooth.
2. Pour the mixture into the Ninja Slushi vessel.
3. Select "SPIKED SLUSH." The preset will start at the default/optimal temperature, which is excellent for the best texture.
4. If you'd like, you can modify the temperature to your preference.
5. When the frozen drink attains the desired temperature, the machine will beep three times.
6. Dispense and enjoy.

Passion Fruit Rum Slushi

Servings: 5-6

Ingredients:

2 cups passion fruit juice

¾ cup dark rum

1 cup sugar

¾ cup light rum

3 tablespoons grenadine syrup

¾ cup lime juice

Preparation:

1. In a large pitcher, combine the fruit juice, rum, sugar, lime juice, and grenadine; mix well until the sugar is fully dissolved.
2. Pour the mixture into the Ninja Slushi vessel.
3. Select "SPIKED SLUSH." The preset will start at the default/optimal temperature, which is excellent for the best texture.
4. If you'd like, you can modify the temperature to your preference.
5. When the frozen drink attains the desired temperature, the machine will beep three times.
6. Dispense and enjoy.

Citrus White Wine Slushi

Servings: 4

Ingredients:

2 cups orange juice

1 cup white wine of your choice

1 cup lemon juice

1 cup pineapple chunks

Sugar, to taste

Preparation:

1. Place all the ingredients into a blender and blend until the mixture is smooth.
2. Pour the mixture into the Ninja Slushi vessel.
3. Select "SPIKED SLUSH." The preset will start at the default/optimal temperature, which is excellent for the best texture.
4. If you'd like, you can modify the temperature to your preference.
5. When the frozen drink attains the desired temperature, the machine will beep three times.
6. Dispense and enjoy.

Spiked Pina Rum Slushi

Servings: 4

Ingredients:

2¼ cups pineapple juice, sweetened

1½ cups light rum

1 can (15 ounces) cream of coconut

Preparation:

1. Combine pineapple juice, light rum, and cream of coconut, and whisk until everything is fully mixed.
2. Pour the mixture into the Ninja Slushi vessel.
3. Select "SPIKED SLUSH." The preset will start at the default/optimal temperature, which is excellent for the best texture.
4. If you'd like, you can modify the temperature to your preference.
5. When the frozen drink attains the desired temperature, the machine will beep three times.
6. Dispense and enjoy.

Delicious Pomegranate Gin Slushi

Servings: 4

Ingredients:

3 cups pomegranate juice

1 tablespoon fresh lime juice

1 cup gin

Sugar to taste, if needed

Preparation:

1. Combine all ingredients in a large pitcher and whisk until the sugar is fully dissolved.
2. Pour the mixture into the Ninja Slushi vessel.
3. Select "SPIKED SLUSH." The preset will start at the default/optimal temperature, which is excellent for the best texture.
4. If you'd like, you can modify the temperature to your preference.
5. When the frozen drink attains the desired temperature, the machine will beep three times.
6. Dispense and enjoy.

Paloma Spiked Slushi

Servings: 1-2

Ingredients:

½-ounce lime juice

½ cup sparkling peach citrus soda or grapefruit soda

1½ ounces tequila

A pinch of salt

Preparation:

1. Combine all ingredients in a large pitcher and whisk until the sugar is fully dissolved.
2. Pour the mixture into the Ninja Slushi vessel.
3. Select "SPIKED SLUSH." The preset will start at the default/optimal temperature, which is excellent for the best texture.
4. If you'd like, you can modify the temperature to your preference.
5. When the frozen drink attains the desired temperature, the machine will beep three times.
6. Dispense and enjoy.

Classic Bloody Mary Slushi

Servings: 1-2

Ingredients:

1⅛ teaspoons celery salt

⅛ teaspoon hot pepper sauce

2 ounces vodka

1 tablespoon lemon juice

¾ teaspoon Worcestershire sauce

1 cup tomato juice

1½ teaspoons lime juice

½ teaspoon prepared horseradish, optional

⅛ teaspoon pepper

Preparation:

1. Combine all ingredients in a large pitcher and whisk until everything is fully mixed.
2. Pour the mixture into the Ninja Slushi vessel.
3. Select "SPIKED SLUSH." The preset will start at the default/optimal temperature, which is excellent for the best texture.
4. If you'd like, you can modify the temperature to your preference.
5. When the frozen drink attains the desired temperature, the machine will beep three times.
6. Dispense and enjoy.

Aromatic Martini Slushi

Servings: 1

Ingredients:

½-ounce dry vermouth

3 ounces gin or vodka

Preparation:

1. Combine vermouth and gin or vodka in a large pitcher and whisk until everything is fully mixed.
2. Pour the mixture into the Ninja Slushi vessel.
3. Select "SPIKED SLUSH." The preset will start at the default/optimal temperature, which is excellent for the best texture.
4. If you'd like, you can modify the temperature to your preference.
5. When the frozen drink attains the desired temperature, the machine will beep three times.
6. Dispense and enjoy.

Raspberry Peach Slushi

Servings: 4

Ingredients:

2 cups raspberries

¼ cup sugar

2 cups peaches

¼ cup tequila

¼ cup lime juice

¼ cup triple sec

Preparation:

1. Place all the ingredients into a blender and blend until the mixture is smooth.
2. Pour the mixture into the Ninja Slushi vessel.
3. Select "SPIKED SLUSH." The preset will start at the default/optimal temperature, which is excellent for the best texture.
4. If you'd like, you can modify the temperature to your preference.
5. When the frozen drink attains the desired temperature, the machine will beep three times.
6. Dispense and enjoy.

Refreshing Mojito Slushi

Servings: 1

Ingredients:

½ cup club soda

2 ounces light rum

1 to 2 lime wedges, squeeze the juice

2 mint sprigs

2 teaspoons sugar

Preparation:

1. Place all the ingredients into a blender and blend until the mixture is smooth.
2. Pour the mixture into the Ninja Slushi vessel.
3. Select "SPIKED SLUSH." The preset will start at the default/optimal temperature, which is excellent for the best texture.
4. If you'd like, you can modify the temperature to your preference.
5. When the frozen drink attains the desired temperature, the machine will beep three times.
6. Dispense and enjoy.

Sparkling Berries Slushi

Servings: 4

Ingredients:

2 cups blueberries

1 cup white wine of your choice

2 cups blackberries

1 cup ginger beer soda

Sugar, to taste

Preparation:

1. Place all the ingredients into a blender and blend until the mixture is smooth.
2. Pour the mixture into the Ninja Slushi vessel.
3. Select "SPIKED SLUSH." The preset will start at the default/optimal temperature, which is excellent for the best texture.
4. If you'd like, you can modify the temperature to your preference.
5. When the frozen drink attains the desired temperature, the machine will beep three times.
6. Dispense and enjoy.

Orange Tequila Slushi

Servings: 1

Ingredients:

1½ ounces tequila

1½ teaspoons grenadine syrup

4½ ounces orange juice

Preparation:

1. Combine all ingredients in a large pitcher and whisk until everything is fully mixed.
2. Pour the mixture into the Ninja Slushi vessel.
3. Select "SPIKED SLUSH." The preset will start at the default/optimal temperature, which is excellent for the best texture.
4. If you'd like, you can modify the temperature to your preference.
5. When the frozen drink attains the desired temperature, the machine will beep three times.
6. Dispense and enjoy.

Sangria Red Wine Slushi

Servings: 2

Ingredients:

1 cup red wine

⅓ cup fresh raspberries

⅓ cup frozen strawberries

¼ cup orange-flavored liqueur

1 tablespoon white sugar, or more to taste

⅓ cup blueberries

½ orange, juiced

Preparation:

1. Combine all of the ingredients in a blender and blend until smooth.

2. Pour the mixture into the Ninja Slushi vessel.

3. Select "SPIKED SLUSH." The preset will start at the default/optimal temperature, which is excellent for the best texture.

4. If you prefer, you can adjust the temperature.

5. When the frozen drink attains the desired temperature, the machine will beep three times.

6. Serve immediately and enjoy.

Lemon Strawberry Daiquiri Slushi

Servings: 4-6

Ingredients:

4 oz. fresh strawberries

⅛ cup lime juice

¼ cup lemon-lime flavored carbonated beverage

¾ cup rum

½ cup white sugar

½ cup lemon juice

Preparation:

1. Combine all of the ingredients in a blender and blend until smooth.

2. Pour the mixture into the Ninja Slushi vessel.

3. Select "SPIKED SLUSH." The preset will start at the default/optimal temperature, which is excellent for the best texture.

4. If you prefer, you can adjust the temperature.

5. When the frozen drink attains the desired temperature, the machine will beep three times.

6. Serve immediately and enjoy.

Flavorful Margarita Cocktail Slushi

Servings: 1

Ingredients:

¼ cup Blanco tequila

2 tablespoons freshly squeezed lime juice

1 tablespoon orange liqueur

1 tablespoon sugar

Preparation:

1. Combine all ingredients in a large pitcher and whisk until the sugar is fully dissolved.
2. Pour the mixture into the Ninja Slushi vessel.
3. Select "SPIKED SLUSH." The preset will start at the default/optimal temperature, which is excellent for the best texture.
4. If you prefer, you can adjust the temperature.
5. When the frozen drink attains the desired temperature, the machine will beep three times.
6. Serve immediately and enjoy.

Delicious Mudslide Slushi

Servings: 1

Ingredients:

2 tablespoons Baileys Irish cream

2 tablespoons vodka

3 tablespoons heavy cream

2 tablespoons coffee liqueur

Preparation:

1. Combine all ingredients in a large pitcher and whisk until everything is fully mixed.
2. Pour the mixture into the Ninja Slushi vessel.
3. Select "SPIKED SLUSH." The preset will start at the default/optimal temperature, which is excellent for the best texture.
4. If you prefer, you can adjust the temperature.
5. When the frozen drink attains the desired temperature, the machine will beep three times.
6. Serve immediately and enjoy.

Lime Grapefruit Paloma Slushi

Servings: 1

Ingredients:

1½ tablespoons tequila

3 tablespoons fresh grapefruit juice

1 tablespoon sugar

½ cup grapefruit soda

2 teaspoons fresh lime juice

Preparation:

1. Combine all ingredients in a large pitcher and whisk until the sugar is fully dissolved.
2. Pour the mixture into the Ninja Slushi vessel.
3. Select "SPIKED SLUSH." The preset will start at the default/optimal temperature, which is excellent for the best texture.
4. If you prefer, you can adjust the temperature.
5. When the frozen drink attains the desired temperature, the machine will beep three times.
6. Serve immediately and enjoy.

Mint Blackberry Bourbon Slushi

Servings: 1

Ingredients:

¼ cup bourbon

1 tablespoon of sugar

1 tablespoon lime juice

2-3 blackberries, muddled

6-7 mint leaves, muddled

2 tablespoons club soda

Preparation:

1. Combine all of the ingredients in a blender and blend until smooth.
2. Pour the mixture into the Ninja Slushi vessel.
3. Select "SPIKED SLUSH." The preset will start at the default/optimal temperature, which is excellent for the best texture.
4. If you prefer, you can adjust the temperature.
5. When the frozen drink attains the desired temperature, the machine will beep three times.
6. Serve immediately and enjoy.

Classic Peach Bellini Slushi

Servings: 2

Ingredients:

½ cup champagne   ¼ cup pureed peaches

Preparation:

1. Combine all ingredients in a large pitcher and whisk until everything is fully mixed.
2. Pour the mixture into the Ninja Slushi vessel.
3. Select "SPIKED SLUSH." The preset will start at the default/optimal temperature, which is excellent for the best texture.
4. If you prefer, you can adjust the temperature.
5. When the frozen drink attains the desired temperature, the machine will beep three times.
6. Serve immediately and enjoy.

Vanilla Eggnog Bourbon Slushi

Servings: 5

Ingredients:

4 large eggs   ¾ cup granulated sugar
¼ cup bourbon   1½ teaspoons vanilla extract
4 cups whole milk

Preparation:

1. Put the eggs in a blender and blend for about a minute on high.
2. Combine all ingredients in a large pitcher and whisk until the sugar is fully dissolved.
3. Pour the mixture into the Ninja Slushi vessel.
4. Select "SPIKED SLUSH." The preset will start at the default/optimal temperature, which is excellent for the best texture.
5. If you prefer, you can adjust the temperature.
6. When the frozen drink attains the desired temperature, the machine will beep three times.
7. Serve immediately and enjoy.

Lemonade Spiked Slushi

Servings: 2

Ingredients:

1 cup water, divided, more to taste

1 cup light rum or vodka, more to taste

1 tablespoon granulated sugar

1 large lemon juice

¼ tablespoon grated lemon zest

Preparation:

1. Combine all ingredients in a large pitcher and whisk until the sugar is fully dissolved.
2. Pour the mixture into the Ninja Slushi vessel.
3. Select "SPIKED SLUSH." The preset will start at the default/optimal temperature, which is excellent for the best texture.
4. If you prefer, you can adjust the temperature.
5. When the frozen drink attains the desired temperature, the machine will beep three times.
6. Serve immediately and enjoy.

Refreshing Blue Lagoon Slushi

Servings: 1

Ingredients:

2 tablespoons vodka

¾ cup lemonade

2 tablespoons blue curacao

Preparation:

1. Combine all ingredients in a large pitcher and whisk until everything is fully mixed.
2. Pour the mixture into the Ninja Slushi vessel.
3. Select "SPIKED SLUSH." The preset will start at the default/optimal temperature, which is excellent for the best texture.
4. If you prefer, you can adjust the temperature.
5. When the frozen drink attains the desired temperature, the machine will beep three times.
6. Serve immediately and enjoy.

Mint Watermelon Tequila Slushi

Servings: 4

Ingredients:

¼ cup water

2 tablespoons fresh lime juice

3 tablespoons granulated sugar

¼ cup lightly packed fresh mint leaves

2 calamansi limes, juice only, optional

4 cups seedless watermelon, diced

½ cup silver tequila

Preparation:

1. Combine all of the ingredients in a blender and blend until smooth.

2. Pour the mixture into the Ninja Slushi vessel.

3. Select "SPIKED SLUSH." The preset will start at the default/optimal temperature, which is excellent for the best texture.

4. If you prefer, you can adjust the temperature.

5. When the frozen drink attains the desired temperature, the machine will beep three times.

6. Serve immediately and enjoy.

Tasty Mai Tai Slushi

Servings: 2

Ingredients:

½ cup pineapple juice

1 teaspoon grenadine syrup

1 (1.5 fluid ounce) jigger spiced rum

¼ cup orange juice

½ (1.5 fluid ounce) jigger coconut-flavored rum

Preparation:

1. Combine all ingredients in a large pitcher and whisk until everything is fully mixed.

2. Pour the mixture into the Ninja Slushi vessel.

3. Select "SPIKED SLUSH." The preset will start at the default/optimal temperature, which is excellent for the best texture.

4. If you prefer, you can adjust the temperature.

5. When the frozen drink attains the desired temperature, the machine will beep three times.

6. Serve immediately and enjoy.

Tropical Rum Slushi

Servings: 4

Ingredients:

3½ cups Orange Pineapple juice

2 tablespoons grenadine

⅓ cup Rum

1-2 limes juice

2 tablespoons simple syrup

Preparation:

1. Combine all ingredients in a large pitcher and whisk until everything is fully mixed.
2. Pour the mixture into the Ninja Slushi vessel.
3. Select "SPIKED SLUSH." The preset will start at the default/optimal temperature, which is excellent for the best texture.
4. If you prefer, you can adjust the temperature.
5. When the frozen drink attains the desired temperature, the machine will beep three times.
6. Serve immediately and enjoy.

Lemon Cucumber Gin Slushi

Servings: 2

Ingredients:

½ cup gin

1 tablespoon sugar

¼ cup fresh lemon juice

½ cup fresh cucumber juice

Preparation:

1. Combine all ingredients in a large pitcher and whisk until the sugar is fully dissolved.
2. Pour the mixture into the Ninja Slushi vessel.
3. Select "SPIKED SLUSH." The preset will start at the default/optimal temperature, which is excellent for the best texture.
4. If you prefer, you can adjust the temperature.
5. When the frozen drink attains the desired temperature, the machine will beep three times.
6. Serve immediately and enjoy.

Lime Cranberry Vodka Slushi

Servings: 2

 Ingredients:

¼ cup vodka

1 lime wedge

½ cup cranberry juice

1 tablespoon sugar

Preparation:

1. Combine all ingredients in a large pitcher and whisk until the sugar is fully dissolved.
2. Pour the mixture into the Ninja Slushi vessel.
3. Select "SPIKED SLUSH." The preset will start at the default/optimal temperature, which is excellent for the best texture.
4. If you prefer, you can adjust the temperature.
5. When the frozen drink attains the desired temperature, the machine will beep three times.
6. Serve immediately and enjoy.

Pineapple Colada Slushi

Servings:

Ingredients:

¼ cup pineapple juice

¼ cup light rum

1 tablespoon freshly squeezed lime juice

¼ cup cream of coconut

2 tablespoons sugar

Preparation:

1. Combine all ingredients in a large pitcher and whisk until the sugar is fully dissolved.
2. Pour the mixture into the Ninja Slushi vessel.
3. Select "SPIKED SLUSH." The preset will start at the default/optimal temperature, which is excellent for the best texture.
4. If you prefer, you can adjust the temperature.
5. When the frozen drink attains the desired temperature, the machine will beep three times.
6. Serve immediately and enjoy.

Passion Fruit Cocktail Slushi

Servings: 2

Ingredients:

¼ cup dark rum

2 tablespoons lime juice, freshly squeezed

1 tablespoon passion fruit puree

¼ cup light rum

2 tablespoons orange juice, freshly squeezed

1 teaspoon grenadine

2 tablespoons simple syrup

Preparation:

1. Combine all ingredients in a large pitcher and whisk until everything is fully mixed.
2. Pour the mixture into the Ninja Slushi vessel.
3. Select "SPIKED SLUSH." The preset will start at the default/optimal temperature, which is excellent for the best texture.
4. If you prefer, you can adjust the temperature.
5. When the frozen drink attains the desired temperature, the machine will beep three times.
6. Serve immediately and enjoy.

Lime Gin and Tonic Slushi

Servings: 1

Ingredients:

¼ cup gin

1 tablespoon fresh lime juice

½ cup tonic water

Preparation:

1. Combine all ingredients in a large pitcher and whisk until everything is fully mixed.
2. Pour the mixture into the Ninja Slushi vessel.
3. Select "SPIKED SLUSH." The preset will start at the default/optimal temperature, which is excellent for the best texture.
4. If you prefer, you can adjust the temperature.
5. When the frozen drink attains the desired temperature, the machine will beep three times.
6. Serve immediately and enjoy.

Sparkling Peach White Wine Slushi

Servings: 5

Ingredients:

1 cup sparkling peach water

½ cup simply peach juice, chilled

2 tablespoons fresh lemon juice

3 cups white wine, sweet or dry

Preparation:

1.Combine all ingredients in a large pitcher and whisk until everything is fully mixed.

2.Pour the mixture into the Ninja Slushi vessel.

3.Select "SPIKED SLUSH." The preset will start at the default/optimal temperature, which is excellent for the best texture.

4.If you prefer, you can adjust the temperature.

5.When the frozen drink attains the desired temperature, the machine will beep three times.

6.Serve immediately and enjoy.

Chapter 3 Frappe Slushies

56 Flavorful Vanilla Frappe Slushi

56 Vanilla Chocolate Frappe Slushi

57 Lime Yogurt Frappe Slushi

57 Espresso Chocolate Frappe Slushi

58 Strawberry Frappe Slushi

58 Matcha Frappe Slushi

59 The Best Tiramisu Frappe Slushi

59 Oreo and Cream Frappe Slushi

60 Creamy Mango Frappe Slushi

60 Cocoa Frappe Slushi

61 Pumpkin Frappe Slushi

61 Fresh Strawberry Frappe Slushi

62 Homemade Caramel Frappe Slushi

62 Raspberry and Cookies Frappe Slushi

63 Vanilla Frappé Slushi

63 Cinnamon Hazelnut Frappé Slushi

64 Green Tea Frappe Slushi

64 Chocolate Frappé Slushi

65 Vanilla Strawberry Frappé Slushi

65 Smooth Double Chocolate Frappé Slushi

66 Vanilla Matcha Green Tea Frappé Slushi

66 Delicious Mango Frappé Slushi

67 Raspberry White Chocolate Frappé Slushi

67 Caramel Tiramisu Frappé Slushi

68 Walnut Oatmeal Frappé Slushi

68 Whiskey Frappé Slushi

69 Simple Coconut Frappé Slushi

69 Blueberry Frappé Slushi

Flavorful Vanilla Frappe Slushi

Servings: 1

Ingredients:

½ cup milk

1.5 tablespoons coffee

1 cup water

¼ teaspoon vanilla essence

2 tablespoons sugar

¼ teaspoon vanilla-flavored powder

Preparation:

1. Combine all ingredients in a large pitcher and whisk until the sugar is fully dissolved.
2. Pour the mixture into the Ninja Slushi vessel.
3. Select "FRAPPE." The preset will start at the default/optimal temperature.
4. Adjust the temperature control to illuminate 4 bars.
5. When the frozen drink attains the desired temperature, the machine will beep three times.
6. Dispense and enjoy.

Vanilla Chocolate Frappe Slushi

Servings: 2

Ingredients:

⅓ cup chocolate chips

2 cups milk

4 tablespoons chocolate syrup

1 teaspoon vanilla essence

4 tablespoons sugar

Preparation:

1. Place all the ingredients into a blender and blend until the mixture is smooth.
2. Pour the mixture into the Ninja Slushi vessel.
3. Select "FRAPPE." The preset will start at the default/optimal temperature.
4. Adjust the temperature control to illuminate 4 bars.
5. When the frozen drink attains the desired temperature, the machine will beep three times.
6. Dispense and enjoy.

Lime Yogurt Frappe Slushi

Servings: 2

Ingredients:

¼ cup milk of your choice

2 teaspoons graham cracker crumbs

½ teaspoon lime peel, grated

2 tablespoons lime juice

2 cups vanilla yogurt

Sugar, to taste

Preparation:

1. In a blender, combine the lime juice, graham cracker crumbs, milk, sugar, yogurt, and lime peel.

2. Process until completely blended.

3. Pour the mixture into the Ninja Slushi vessel.

4. Select "FRAPPE." The preset will start at the default/optimal temperature.

5. Adjust the temperature control to illuminate 4 bars.

6. When the frozen drink attains the desired temperature, the machine will beep three times.

7. Dispense and enjoy.

Espresso Chocolate Frappe Slushi

Servings: 1

Ingredients:

1 tablespoon granulated white sugar

2 shots espresso

1 tablespoon chocolate syrup

½ cup milk

½ cup cream (whipped)

Preparation:

1. Combine all ingredients in a large pitcher and whisk until the sugar is fully dissolved.

2. Pour the mixture into the Ninja Slushi vessel.

3. Select "FRAPPE." The preset will start at the default/optimal temperature.

4. Adjust the temperature control to illuminate 4 bars.

5. When the frozen drink attains the desired temperature, the machine will beep three times.

6. Dispense and enjoy.

Strawberry Frappe Slushi

Servings: 1-2

Ingredients:

1 cup brewed coffee, room temperature

¼ teaspoon almond extract

½ cup milk

2 tablespoons vanilla frosting

¼ cup strawberry syrup

2 tablespoons sugar

Preparation:

1. Combine all ingredients in a large pitcher and whisk until the sugar is fully dissolved.
2. Pour the mixture into the Ninja Slushi vessel.
3. Select "FRAPPE." The preset will start at the default/optimal temperature.
4. Adjust the temperature control to illuminate 4 bars.
5. When the frozen drink attains the desired temperature, the machine will beep three times.
6. Dispense and enjoy.

Matcha Frappe Slushi

Servings: 1-2

Ingredients:

1 cup milk

1 tablespoon matcha

Sugar, to taste

4 drops vanilla essence

1 cup ice cream

Preparation:

1. Combine all ingredients in a large pitcher and whisk until the sugar is fully dissolved.
2. Pour the mixture into the Ninja Slushi vessel.
3. Select "FRAPPE." The preset will start at the default/optimal temperature.
4. Adjust the temperature control to illuminate 4 bars.
5. When the frozen drink attains the desired temperature, the machine will beep three times.
6. Dispense and enjoy.

The Best Tiramisu Frappe Slushi

Servings: 1

Ingredients:

¾ glass milk

1 teaspoon coffee

1 tablespoon cream cheese

4 tablespoons condensed milk

2 scoops chocolate ice cream

1 chocolate cupcake

Preparation:

1. Place all the ingredients into a blender and blend until the mixture is smooth.
2. Pour the mixture into the Ninja Slushi vessel.
3. Select "FRAPPE." The preset will start at the default/optimal temperature.
4. Adjust the temperature control to illuminate 4 bars.
5. When the frozen drink attains the desired temperature, the machine will beep three times.
6. Dispense and enjoy.

Oreo and Cream Frappe Slushi

Servings: 2

Ingredients:

1 cup milk

8-10 Oreo cookies

1 packet coffee creamer

½ cup cream

3 tablespoons powdered chocolate

4-6 scoops vanilla ice cream

1 cup black coffee

1 tablespoon sugar

Preparation:

1. Place all the ingredients into a blender and blend until the mixture is smooth.
2. Pour the mixture into the Ninja Slushi vessel.
3. Select "FRAPPE." The preset will start at the default/optimal temperature.
4. Adjust the temperature control to illuminate 4 bars.
5. When the frozen drink attains the desired temperature, the machine will beep three times.
6. Dispense and enjoy.

Creamy Mango Frappe Slushi

Servings: 1

Ingredients:

1 mango, chunks

½ cup fresh cream

1 cup milk

1 tablespoon powdered sugar

Preparation:

1. Place all the ingredients into a blender and blend until the mixture is smooth.
2. Pour the mixture into the Ninja Slushi vessel.
3. Select "FRAPPE." The preset will start at the default/optimal temperature.
4. Adjust the temperature control to illuminate 4 bars.
5. When the frozen drink attains the desired temperature, the machine will beep three times.
6. Dispense and enjoy.

Cocoa Frappe Slushi

Servings: 1-2

Ingredients:

2 tablespoons sugar

¾ cup brewed coffee

1½ cups milk

¼ cup cocoa powder

Preparation:

1. Combine all ingredients in a large pitcher and whisk until the sugar is fully dissolved.
2. Pour the mixture into the Ninja Slushi vessel.
3. Select "FRAPPE." The preset will start at the default/optimal temperature.
4. Adjust the temperature control to illuminate 4 bars.
5. When the frozen drink attains the desired temperature, the machine will beep three times.
6. Dispense and enjoy.

Pumpkin Frappe Slushi

Servings: 2

Ingredients:

1½ cups black coffee

¼ cup pumpkin puree

1¼ cups vanilla almond milk, or any milk

¼ teaspoon ground cloves

3 tablespoons sugar

¼ teaspoon ground nutmeg

1 teaspoon ground cinnamon

½ teaspoon pumpkin spice

Preparation:

1. Place all the ingredients into a blender and blend until the mixture is smooth.
2. Pour the mixture into the Ninja Slushi vessel.
3. Select "FRAPPE." The preset will start at the default/optimal temperature.
4. Adjust the temperature control to illuminate 4 bars.
5. When the frozen drink attains the desired temperature, the machine will beep three times.
6. Dispense and enjoy.

Fresh Strawberry Frappe Slushi

Servings: 1

Ingredients:

¼ cup strawberry ice cream

½ cup milk

1 tablespoon sugar

6-7 strawberries

Half banana (optional)

Preparation:

1. Place all the ingredients into a blender and blend until the mixture is smooth.
2. Pour the mixture into the Ninja Slushi vessel.
3. Select "FRAPPE." The preset will start at the default/optimal temperature.
4. Adjust the temperature control to illuminate 4 bars.
5. When the frozen drink attains the desired temperature, the machine will beep three times.
6. Dispense and enjoy.

Homemade Caramel Frappe Slushi

Servings: 1-2

Ingredients:

1 cup strong brewed coffee

2 tablespoons sugar

½ cup caramel sauce

1 cup milk

Preparation:

1. Combine all ingredients in a large pitcher and whisk until the sugar is fully dissolved.
2. Pour the mixture into the Ninja Slushi vessel.
3. Select "FRAPPE." The preset will start at the default/optimal temperature.
4. Adjust the temperature control to illuminate 4 bars.
5. When the frozen drink attains the desired temperature, the machine will beep three times.
6. Dispense and enjoy.

Raspberry and Cookies Frappe Slushi

Servings: 1

Ingredients:

1½ cups raspberries

¼ cup milk

3 tablespoons milk

1 chocolate bar

2 cups raspberry ice cream

⅓ cup crushed shortbread cookies

1 tablespoon seedless raspberry jam

Preparation:

1. Place all the ingredients into a blender and blend until the mixture is smooth.
2. Pour the mixture into the Ninja Slushi vessel.
3. Select "FRAPPE." The preset will start at the default/optimal temperature.
4. Adjust the temperature control to illuminate 4 bars.
5. When the frozen drink attains the desired temperature, the machine will beep three times.
6. Dispense and enjoy.

Vanilla Frappé Slushi

Servings: 1

Ingredients:

1½ cups milk

1 cup brewed coffee

1 teaspoon sugar

3 scoops vanilla bean ice cream

⅛ teaspoon vanilla extract

Preparation:

1. Combine all ingredients in a large pitcher and whisk until the sugar is fully dissolved.
2. Pour the mixture into the Ninja Slushi vessel.
3. Select "FRAPPE." The preset will start at the default/optimal temperature.
4. Adjust the temperature control to illuminate 4 bars.
5. When the frozen drink attains the desired temperature, the machine will beep three times.
6. Serve immediately and enjoy.

Cinnamon Hazelnut Frappé Slushi

Servings: 2

Ingredients:

1 cup strong coffee

2 tablespoons hazelnut syrup

2 cups unsweetened almond milk

Dash of ground cinnamon

2 tablespoons sugar

Preparation:

1. Combine all ingredients in a large pitcher and whisk until the sugar is fully dissolved.
2. Pour the mixture into the Ninja Slushi vessel.
3. Select "FRAPPE." The preset will start at the default/optimal temperature.
4. Adjust the temperature control to illuminate 4 bars.
5. When the frozen drink attains the desired temperature, the machine will beep three times.
6. Serve immediately and enjoy.

Green Tea Frappe Slushi

Servings: 4

Ingredients:

¾ cup sweetened condensed milk

3 green tea bags

1 cup ice cream

1 cup boiling water

½ cup milk

Preparation:

1. Put tea bags in a small bowl.

2. Add boiling water.

3. Let stand for 15 minutes or until completely cooled

4. Discard tea bags.

5. Combine all ingredients in a large pitcher and whisk until everything is fully mixed.

6. Pour the mixture into the Ninja Slushi vessel.

7. Select "FRAPPE." The preset will start at the default/optimal temperature.

8. Adjust the temperature control to illuminate 4 bars.

9. When the frozen drink attains the desired temperature, the machine will beep three times.

10. Dispense and enjoy.

Chocolate Frappé Slushi

Servings: 5

Ingredients:

2 cups brewed coffee, cooled

3½ tablespoons chocolate syrup

2 cups dairy milk

3½ tablespoons granulated sugar

Preparation:

1. Combine all ingredients in a large pitcher and whisk until the sugar is fully dissolved.

2. Pour the mixture into the Ninja Slushi vessel.

3. Select "FRAPPE." The preset will start at the default/optimal temperature.

4. Adjust the temperature control to illuminate 4 bars.

5. When the frozen drink attains the desired temperature, the machine will beep three times.

6. Serve immediately and enjoy.

Vanilla Strawberry Frappé Slushi

Servings: 2

Ingredients:

1 cup whole milk

1 tablespoon sugar

2 cups strawberries, stems removed

1 teaspoon vanilla extract

½ cup vanilla ice cream

1 cup brewed coffee, at room temperature

Preparation:

1. Combine all of the ingredients in a blender and blend until smooth.
2. Pour the mixture into the Ninja Slushi vessel.
3. Select "FRAPPE." The preset will start at the default/optimal temperature.
4. Adjust the temperature control to illuminate 4 bars.
5. When the frozen drink attains the desired temperature, the machine will beep three times.
6. Serve immediately and enjoy.

Smooth Double Chocolate Frappé Slushi

Servings: 1

Ingredients:

1 cup milk

¼ cup mini chocolate chips

1 teaspoon vanilla extract

2 tablespoons sugar

3 tablespoons chocolate syrup, divided use

1 cup strong coffee

Preparation:

1. Combine all of the ingredients in a blender and blend until smooth.
2. Pour the mixture into the Ninja Slushi vessel.
3. Select "FRAPPE." The preset will start at the default/optimal temperature.
4. Adjust the temperature control to illuminate 4 bars.
5. When the frozen drink attains the desired temperature, the machine will beep three times.
6. Serve immediately and enjoy.

Vanilla Matcha Green Tea Frappé Slushi

Servings: 2

Ingredients:

¾ cup whole milk

1 tablespoon matcha green tea powder

¼ cup heavy cream

1 tablespoon of sugar

¼ teaspoon of pure vanilla extract

1 tablespoon vanilla-flavored syrup

Preparation:

1. Combine all ingredients in a large pitcher and whisk until the sugar is fully dissolved.
2. Pour the mixture into the Ninja Slushi vessel.
3. Select "FRAPPE." The preset will start at the default/optimal temperature.
4. Adjust the temperature control to illuminate 4 bars.
5. When the frozen drink attains the desired temperature, the machine will beep three times.
6. Serve immediately and enjoy.

Delicious Mango Frappé Slushi

Servings: 2

Ingredients:

2 mangoes

1 cup milk

3 tablespoons sugar or to taste

½ cup strongly brewed coffee

Preparation:

1. Combine all of the ingredients in a blender and blend until smooth.
2. Pour the mixture into the Ninja Slushi vessel.
3. Select "FRAPPE." The preset will start at the default/optimal temperature.
4. Adjust the temperature control to illuminate 4 bars.
5. When the frozen drink attains the desired temperature, the machine will beep three times.
6. Serve immediately and enjoy.

Raspberry White Chocolate Frappé Slushi

Servings: 1

Ingredients:

¾ cup strongly brewed coffee

4 tablespoons raspberry syrup

6 tablespoons white chocolate sauce

⅔ cup whole milk

1 tablespoon sugar

Preparation:

1. Combine all ingredients in a large pitcher and whisk until the sugar is fully dissolved.
2. Pour the mixture into the Ninja Slushi vessel.
3. Select "FRAPPE." The preset will start at the default/optimal temperature.
4. Adjust the temperature control to illuminate 4 bars.
5. When the frozen drink attains the desired temperature, the machine will beep three times.
6. Serve immediately and enjoy.

Caramel Tiramisu Frappé Slushi

Servings: 1

Ingredients:

¼ cup coffee

1 tablespoon vanilla syrup

½ cup whole milk

2 tablespoons chocolate syrup

1 teaspoon espresso powder

2 tablespoons caramel sauce

½ teaspoon cocoa powder

1 teaspoon hazelnut extract

1 teaspoon sugar

Preparation:

1. Combine all ingredients in a large pitcher and whisk until the sugar is fully dissolved.
2. Pour the mixture into the Ninja Slushi vessel.
3. Select "FRAPPE." The preset will start at the default/optimal temperature.
4. Adjust the temperature control to illuminate 4 bars.
5. When the frozen drink attains the desired temperature, the machine will beep three times.
6. Serve immediately and enjoy.

Walnut Oatmeal Frappé Slushi

Servings: 1

Ingredients:

½ teaspoon ground cinnamon

2 tablespoons rolled oats

¾ cup unsweetened almond milk

1 cup strong coffee

4 walnuts

1 medjool date, pitted and rough chopped

1-2 teaspoons sugar

Preparation:

1. Combine all of the ingredients in a blender and blend until smooth.
2. Pour the mixture into the Ninja Slushi vessel.
3. Select "FRAPPE." The preset will start at the default/optimal temperature.
4. Adjust the temperature control to illuminate 4 bars.
5. When the frozen drink attains the desired temperature, the machine will beep three times.
6. Serve immediately and enjoy.

Whiskey Frappé Slushi

Servings: 2

Ingredients:

1 cup strong coffee

2 tablespoon Irish whiskey

½ cup half and half

2 tablespoons brown sugar

Preparation:

1. Combine all ingredients in a large pitcher and whisk until everything is fully mixed.
2. Pour the mixture into the Ninja Slushi vessel.
3. Select "FRAPPE." The preset will start at the default/optimal temperature.
4. Adjust the temperature control to illuminate 4 bars.
5. When the frozen drink attains the desired temperature, the machine will beep three times.
6. Serve immediately and enjoy.

Simple Coconut Frappé Slushi

Servings: 1

Ingredients:

1 cup brewed coffee, cooled

3 tablespoons cream of coconut

1 tablespoon sugar

¼ cup coconut milk

Preparation:

1. Combine all ingredients in a large pitcher and whisk until the sugar is fully dissolved.
2. Pour the mixture into the Ninja Slushi vessel.
3. Select "FRAPPE." The preset will start at the default/optimal temperature.
4. Adjust the temperature control to illuminate 4 bars.
5. When the frozen drink attains the desired temperature, the machine will beep three times.
6. Serve immediately and enjoy.

Blueberry Frappé Slushi

Servings: 2

Ingredients:

2 tablespoons blueberry cobbler Syrup

1 tablespoon sugar

½ cup milk of your choice

1 cup brewed coffee, cooled

Preparation:

1. Combine all ingredients in a large pitcher and whisk until the sugar is fully dissolved.
2. Pour the mixture into the Ninja Slushi vessel.
3. Select "FRAPPE." The preset will start at the default/optimal temperature.
4. Adjust the temperature control to illuminate 4 bars.
5. When the frozen drink attains the desired temperature, the machine will beep three times.
6. Serve immediately and enjoy.

Chapter 4 Milkshake Slushies

71 Banana Chocolate Chip Vanilla Milkshake Slushi

71 Peanut Butter Vanilla Milkshake Slushi

72 Chocolate Cookie-Kahlua Milkshake Slushi

72 Cinnamon Apple Shake Slushi

73 Simple Brownie Milkshake Slushi

73 Pineapple Milkshake Slushi

74 Salted Caramel Vanilla Milkshake Slushi

74 Banana Date Milkshake Slushi

75 Banana Oats Milkshake Slushi

75 Mint Chocolate Chip Vanilla Milkshake Slushi

76 Walnut Milkshake Slushi

76 Vanilla Blueberry Milkshake Slushi

77 KitKat Vanilla Milkshake Slushi

77 Cream Cheese Milkshake Slushi

78 Easy Butterscotch Milkshake Slushi

78 Vanilla Milkshake Slushi

79 Creamy Banana Nutella Milkshake Slushi

79 Chocolate Peanut Butter Milkshake Slushi

80 Caramel Pretzel Milkshake Slushi

80 Almond Chocolate Milkshake Slushi

81 Oreo Vanilla Milkshake Slushi

81 Pumpkin Milkshake Slushi

82 Orange Vanilla Milkshake Slushi

82 Coconut Pineapple Milkshake Slushi

83 Mint Chocolate Milkshake Slushi

83 Cinnamon Peach Milkshake Slushi

84 Homemade Chocolate Hazelnut Milkshake Slushi

Banana Chocolate Chip Vanilla Milkshake Slushi

Servings: 2

Ingredients:

3 cups vanilla ice cream

2 bananas, peeled

½ cup whole milk

⅛ teaspoon vanilla extract

2 tablespoons sugar

½ cup mini chocolate chips

Preparation:

1. Place all the ingredients into a blender and blend until the mixture is smooth.
2. Pour the mixture into the Ninja Slushi vessel.
3. Select "MILKSHAKE." The preset will start at the default/optimal temperature, which is excellent for the best texture.
4. If you'd like, you can modify the temperature to your preference.
5. When the frozen drink attains the desired temperature, the machine will beep three times.
6. Dispense and enjoy.

Peanut Butter Vanilla Milkshake Slushi

Servings: 2

Ingredients:

½ cup whole milk

3 cups vanilla ice cream

½ cup creamy peanut butter

1 pinch kosher salt

⅛ teaspoon vanilla extract

2 tablespoons sugar

Preparation:

1. Place all the ingredients into a blender and blend until the mixture is smooth.
2. Pour the mixture into the Ninja Slushi vessel.
3. Select "MILKSHAKE." The preset will start at the default/optimal temperature, which is excellent for the best texture.
4. If you'd like, you can modify the temperature to your preference.
5. When the frozen drink attains the desired temperature, the machine will beep three times.
6. Dispense and enjoy.

Chocolate Cookie-Kahlua Milkshake Slushi

Servings: 2

Ingredients:

4 tablespoons Kahlua

5 scoops coffee ice-cream

2 chocolate chip cookies, chopped roughly

1½ cups milk of your choice

2 tablespoons sugar

Preparation:

1. Place all the ingredients into a blender and blend until the mixture is smooth.
2. Pour the mixture into the Ninja Slushi vessel.
3. Select "MILKSHAKE." The preset will start at the default/optimal temperature, which is excellent for the best texture.
4. If you'd like, you can modify the temperature to your preference.
5. When the frozen drink attains the desired temperature, the machine will beep three times.
6. Dispense and enjoy.

Cinnamon Apple Shake Slushi

Servings: 2

Ingredients:

1 cup skin-peeled apples, chopped roughly

2 tablespoons sugar

2 cups milk of your choice

4 almonds (optional)

1 teaspoon cinnamon powder

Preparation:

1. Place all the ingredients into a blender and blend until the mixture is smooth.
2. Pour the mixture into the Ninja Slushi vessel.
3. Select "MILKSHAKE." The preset will start at the default/optimal temperature, which is excellent for the best texture.
4. If you'd like, you can modify the temperature to your preference.
5. When the frozen drink attains the desired temperature, the machine will beep three times.
6. Dispense and enjoy.

Simple Brownie Milkshake Slushi

Servings: 2

Ingredients:

½ cup whole milk

3 cups vanilla ice cream (you can also use chocolate ice cream)

1 cup chopped brownie pieces

2 tablespoons sugar

⅛ teaspoon vanilla extract

Preparation:

1. Place all the ingredients into a blender and blend until the mixture is smooth.
2. Pour the mixture into the Ninja Slushi vessel.
3. Select "MILKSHAKE." The preset will start at the default/optimal temperature, which is excellent for the best texture.
4. If you'd like, you can modify the temperature to your preference.
5. When the frozen drink attains the desired temperature, the machine will beep three times.
6. Dispense and enjoy.

Pineapple Milkshake Slushi

Servings: 3

Ingredients:

3 scoops vanilla frozen yogurt or ice-cream

1 box of pineapple cake mix

4 cups milk

2 cups pineapple

3 to 4 tablespoons sugar

Preparation:

1. Place all the ingredients into a blender and blend until the mixture is smooth.
2. Pour the mixture into the Ninja Slushi vessel.
3. Select "MILKSHAKE." The preset will start at the default/optimal temperature, which is excellent for the best texture.
4. If you'd like, you can modify the temperature to your preference.
5. When the frozen drink attains the desired temperature, the machine will beep three times.
6. Dispense and enjoy.

Salted Caramel Vanilla Milkshake Slushi

Servings: 2

Ingredients:

4 cups vanilla ice cream

¼ cup salted caramel sauce

½ cup whipped cream

1 cup milk

2 tablespoons sugar

Preparation:

1. Combine all ingredients in a large pitcher and whisk until the sugar is fully dissolved.
2. Pour the mixture into the Ninja Slushi vessel.
3. Select "MILKSHAKE." The preset will start at the default/optimal temperature, which is excellent for the best texture.
4. If you'd like, you can modify the temperature to your preference.
5. When the frozen drink attains the desired temperature, the machine will beep three times.
6. Dispense and enjoy.

Banana Date Milkshake Slushi

Servings: 1

Ingredients:

2 cups whole milk

½ teaspoon cinnamon

4 pitted Medjool dates – chopped

1 teaspoon flaxseeds

1 banana, chopped

1 scoop vanilla ice-cream

Preparation:

1. Place all the ingredients into a blender and blend until the mixture is smooth.
2. Pour the mixture into the Ninja Slushi vessel.
3. Select "MILKSHAKE." The preset will start at the default/optimal temperature, which is excellent for the best texture.
4. If you'd like, you can modify the temperature to your preference.
5. When the frozen drink attains the desired temperature, the machine will beep three times.
6. Dispense and enjoy.

Banana Oats Milkshake Slushi

Servings: 2

Ingredients:

2 teaspoons rolled oats

2 cups of almond milk

1 tablespoon flax seeds

3 tablespoons peanut butter

1 chopped and frozen banana

2 tablespoons sugar

Preparation:

1. Place all the ingredients into a blender and blend until the mixture is smooth.
2. Pour the mixture into the Ninja Slushi vessel.
3. Select "MILKSHAKE." The preset will start at the default/optimal temperature, which is excellent for the best texture.
4. If you'd like, you can modify the temperature to your preference.
5. When the frozen drink attains the desired temperature, the machine will beep three times.
6. Dispense and enjoy.

Mint Chocolate Chip Vanilla Milkshake Slushi

Servings: 2

Ingredients:

3 cups vanilla ice cream

1 cup whole milk

$\frac{1}{8}$ teaspoon peppermint extract

$\frac{1}{2}$ cup mini chocolate chips

Sugar, to taste

Preparation:

1. Place all the ingredients into a blender and blend until the mixture is smooth.
2. Pour the mixture into the Ninja Slushi vessel.
3. Select "MILKSHAKE." The preset will start at the default/optimal temperature, which is excellent for the best texture.
4. If you'd like, you can modify the temperature to your preference.
5. When the frozen drink attains the desired temperature, the machine will beep three times.
6. Dispense and enjoy.

Walnut Milkshake Slushi

Servings: 2

Ingredients:

3 cups vanilla ice cream

½ cup chopped walnuts

⅛ teaspoon vanilla extract

1 cup whole milk

¼ teaspoon ground cinnamon

Preparation:

1. Place all the ingredients into a blender and blend until the mixture is smooth.
2. Pour the mixture into the Ninja Slushi vessel.
3. Select "MILKSHAKE." The preset will start at the default/optimal temperature, which is excellent for the best texture.
4. If you'd like, you can modify the temperature to your preference.
5. When the frozen drink attains the desired temperature, the machine will beep three times.
6. Dispense and enjoy.

Vanilla Blueberry Milkshake Slushi

Servings: 1

Ingredients:

½ cup whole milk

⅛ teaspoon vanilla extract

1 cup blueberries plus extra 2 for garnish

3 cups vanilla ice cream

Sugar, to taste

Preparation:

1. Place all the ingredients into a blender and blend until the mixture is smooth.
2. Pour the mixture into the Ninja Slushi vessel.
3. Select "MILKSHAKE." The preset will start at the default/optimal temperature, which is excellent for the best texture.
4. If you'd like, you can modify the temperature to your preference.
5. When the frozen drink attains the desired temperature, the machine will beep three times.
6. Dispense and enjoy.

KitKat Vanilla Milkshake Slushi

Servings: 2

Ingredients:

2 KitKat bars

1 teaspoon vanilla essence

2 cups vanilla ice cream

1 cup milk

Sugar to taste

1 tablespoon chocolate syrup

Preparation:

1. Place all the ingredients into a blender and blend until the mixture is smooth.

2. Pour the mixture into the Ninja Slushi vessel.

3. Select "MILKSHAKE." The preset will start at the default/optimal temperature, which is excellent for the best texture.

4. If you'd like, you can modify the temperature to your preference.

5. When the frozen drink attains the desired temperature, the machine will beep three times.

6. Dispense and enjoy.

Cream Cheese Milkshake Slushi

Servings: 1

Ingredients:

3 cups vanilla ice cream

½ cup whole milk

½ cup cream cheese

2 tablespoons graham cracker crumbs

⅛ teaspoon vanilla extract

Preparation:

1. Place all the ingredients into a blender and blend until the mixture is smooth.

2. Pour the mixture into the Ninja Slushi vessel.

3. Select "MILKSHAKE." The preset will start at the default/optimal temperature, which is excellent for the best texture.

4. If you'd like, you can modify the temperature to your preference.

5. When the frozen drink attains the desired temperature, the machine will beep three times.

6. Dispense and enjoy.

Easy Butterscotch Milkshake Slushi

Servings: 2

Ingredients:

1 scoop butterscotch ice cream

2 teaspoons butterscotch sauce

1 cup milk

2 teaspoons butterscotch chips

Sugar, to taste

Preparation:

1. Place all the ingredients into a blender and blend until the mixture is smooth.
2. Pour the mixture into the Ninja Slushi vessel.
3. Select "MILKSHAKE." The preset will start at the default/optimal temperature, which is excellent for the best texture.
4. If you'd like, you can modify the temperature to your preference.
5. When the frozen drink attains the desired temperature, the machine will beep three times.
6. Dispense and enjoy.

Vanilla Milkshake Slushi

Servings: 3

Ingredients:

1 cup whole milk

4 cups Vanilla Ice Cream

1 teaspoon vanilla extract or vanilla

essence

2 to 3 teaspoons sugar

Preparation:

1. Combine all of the ingredients in a blender and blend until smooth.
2. Pour the mixture into the Ninja Slushi vessel.
3. Select "MILKSHAKE." The preset will start at the default/optimal temperature, which is excellent for the best texture.
4. If you prefer, you can adjust the temperature.
5. When the frozen drink attains the desired temperature, the machine will beep three times.
6. Serve immediately and enjoy.

Creamy Banana Nutella Milkshake Slushi

Servings: 2

Ingredients:

2 bananas

½ cup heavy cream

4 tablespoons Nutella

1 teaspoon vanilla, optional

1 tablespoon sugar

1 cup milk

Preparation:

1. Combine all of the ingredients in a blender and blend until smooth.

2. Pour the mixture into the Ninja Slushi vessel.

3. Select "MILKSHAKE." The preset will start at the default/optimal temperature, which is excellent for the best texture.

4. If you prefer, you can adjust the temperature.

5. When the frozen drink attains the desired temperature, the machine will beep three times.

6. Serve immediately and enjoy.

Chocolate Peanut Butter Milkshake Slushi

Servings: 2

Ingredients:

⅓ cup smooth peanut butter

2 tablespoons sugar

1 cup milk

2 cups chocolate ice cream

Preparation:

1. Combine all of the ingredients in a blender and blend until smooth.

2. Pour the mixture into the Ninja Slushi vessel.

3. Select "MILKSHAKE." The preset will start at the default/optimal temperature, which is excellent for the best texture.

4. If you prefer, you can adjust the temperature.

5. When the frozen drink attains the desired temperature, the machine will beep three times.

6. Serve immediately and enjoy.

Caramel Pretzel Milkshake Slushi

Servings: 4

Ingredients:

1½ cups vanilla ice cream

10 mini pretzel twists, crushed

2 tablespoons whole milk

1 tablespoon sugar

⅛ teaspoon salt

2 tablespoons caramel sauce

Preparation:

1. Combine all of the ingredients in a blender and blend until smooth.

2. Pour the mixture into the Ninja Slushi vessel.

3. Select "MILKSHAKE." The preset will start at the default/optimal temperature, which is excellent for the best texture.

4. If you prefer, you can adjust the temperature.

5. When the frozen drink attains the desired temperature, the machine will beep three times.

6. Serve immediately and enjoy.

Almond Chocolate Milkshake Slushi

Servings: 2

Ingredients:

4 cups chocolate ice cream

¼ cup milk

1 tablespoon coffee

2 Hershey's Almonds chocolate bars, chopped

1 tablespoon sugar

Preparation:

1. Combine all of the ingredients in a blender and blend until smooth.

2. Pour the mixture into the Ninja Slushi vessel.

3. Select "MILKSHAKE." The preset will start at the default/optimal temperature, which is excellent for the best texture.

4. If you prefer, you can adjust the temperature.

5. When the frozen drink attains the desired temperature, the machine will beep three times.

6. Serve immediately and enjoy.

Oreo Vanilla Milkshake Slushi

Servings: 2

Ingredients:

6 chocolate sandwich cookies, like Oreo

¾ cup milk

3 scoops vanilla ice cream

1 tablespoon sugar

Preparation:

1. Combine all of the ingredients in a blender and blend until smooth.
2. Pour the mixture into the Ninja Slushi vessel.
3. Select "MILKSHAKE." The preset will start at the default/optimal temperature, which is excellent for the best texture.
4. If you prefer, you can adjust the temperature.
5. When the frozen drink attains the desired temperature, the machine will beep three times.
6. Serve immediately and enjoy.

Pumpkin Milkshake Slushi

Servings: 2

Ingredients:

1 cup vanilla ice cream

½ teaspoon Pumpkin Pie spice

⅔ cup milk

1 teaspoon pure vanilla extract

½ cup Pumpkin, solid pack

Preparation:

1. Combine all of the ingredients in a blender and blend until smooth.
2. Pour the mixture into the Ninja Slushi vessel.
3. Select "MILKSHAKE." The preset will start at the default/optimal temperature, which is excellent for the best texture.
4. If you prefer, you can adjust the temperature.
5. When the frozen drink attains the desired temperature, the machine will beep three times.
6. Serve immediately and enjoy.

Orange Vanilla Milkshake Slushi

Servings: 2

Ingredients:

2 large scoops of orange sherbet

¼ cup milk

2 large scoops of vanilla ice cream

½ teaspoon vanilla extract

2 tablespoons orange juice

1 tablespoon sugar

Preparation:

1.Combine all of the ingredients in a blender and blend until smooth.

2.Pour the mixture into the Ninja Slushi vessel.

3.Select "MILKSHAKE." The preset will start at the default/optimal temperature, which is excellent for the best texture.

4.If you prefer, you can adjust the temperature.

5.When the frozen drink attains the desired temperature, the machine will beep three times.

6.Serve immediately and enjoy.

Coconut Pineapple Milkshake Slushi

Servings: 2

Ingredients:

⅓ cup coconut cream

1½ – 2 cups pineapple, chunks

1 small banana

¾ cup coconut ice cream

⅓ cup milk

2 tablespoons sugar

Preparation:

1.Combine all of the ingredients in a blender and blend until smooth.

2.Pour the mixture into the Ninja Slushi vessel.

3.Select "MILKSHAKE." The preset will start at the default/optimal temperature, which is excellent for the best texture.

4.If you prefer, you can adjust the temperature.

5.When the frozen drink attains the desired temperature, the machine will beep three times.

6.Serve immediately and enjoy.

Mint Chocolate Milkshake Slushi

Servings: 2

Ingredients:

3 cups mint chocolate chip ice cream

1 tablespoon dark chocolate syrup

1½ cups whole milk

1½ tablespoons sugar

Preparation:

1. Combine all of the ingredients in a blender and blend until smooth.
2. Pour the mixture into the Ninja Slushi vessel.
3. Select "MILKSHAKE." The preset will start at the default/optimal temperature, which is excellent for the best texture.
4. If you prefer, you can adjust the temperature.
5. When the frozen drink attains the desired temperature, the machine will beep three times.
6. Serve immediately and enjoy.

Cinnamon Peach Milkshake Slushi

Servings: 2

Ingredients:

2 large ripe clean peaches, chopped

1½ cups vanilla ice cream

2 tablespoons sweetened condensed milk

½ teaspoon ground cinnamon

1 teaspoon vanilla extract

½ cup whole milk

1 tablespoon light brown sugar

Preparation:

1. Combine all of the ingredients in a blender and blend until smooth.
2. Pour the mixture into the Ninja Slushi vessel.
3. Select "MILKSHAKE." The preset will start at the default/optimal temperature, which is excellent for the best texture.
4. If you prefer, you can adjust the temperature.
5. When the frozen drink attains the desired temperature, the machine will beep three times.
6. Serve immediately and enjoy.

Homemade Chocolate Hazelnut Milkshake Slushi

Servings: 2

Ingredients:

1 cup cocoa powder

1 cup cream

2 tablespoons hazelnut paste

1 cup milk

1 tablespoon sugar

Preparation:

1. Combine all of the ingredients in a blender and blend until smooth.

2. Pour the mixture into the Ninja Slushi vessel.

3. Select "MILKSHAKE." The preset will start at the default/optimal temperature, which is excellent for the best texture.

4. If you prefer, you can adjust the temperature.

5. When the frozen drink attains the desired temperature, the machine will beep three times.

6. Serve immediately and enjoy.

Chapter 5 Frozen Juice Slushies

86 Carrot Tangerine Frozen Juice Slushi

86 Tropical Mango Pineapple Frozen Juice Slushi

87 Apple Kiwi Frozen Juice Slushi

87 Apple and Cranberry Frozen Juice Slushi

88 Lime Cherry Frozen Juice Slushi

88 Pineapple and Passionfruit Frozen Juice Slushi

89 Orange-Raspberry Frozen Juice Slushi

89 Coconut Pineapple Frozen Juice Slushi

90 Coconut Watermelon Frozen Juice Slushi

90 Blueberry Pomegranate Frozen Juice Slushi

91 Flavorful Passion Fruit Frozen Juice Slushi

91 Easy Black Grapes Frozen Juice Slushi

92 Banana Strawberry Frozen Juice Slushi

92 Cherry Frozen Juice Slushi

93 Orange Pineapple Frozen Juice Slushi

93 Mango Peach Frozen Juice Slushi

94 Simple Orange Frozen Juice Slushi

94 Tropical Fruits Coconut Frozen Juice Slushi

Carrot Tangerine Frozen Juice Slushi

Servings: 4

Ingredients:

2 cups carrot juice (or fresh carrots blended into juice)

2 to 3 tablespoons sugar

2 cups tangerine juice (or fresh tangerines juiced)

Preparation:

1. Combine all ingredients in a large pitcher and whisk until the sugar is fully dissolved.
2. Pour the mixture into the Ninja Slushi vessel.
3. Select "FROZEN JUICE." The preset will start at the default/optimal temperature, which is excellent for the best texture.
4. If you'd like, you can modify the temperature to your preference.
5. When the frozen drink attains the desired temperature, the machine will beep three times.
6. Dispense and enjoy.

Tropical Mango Pineapple Frozen Juice Slushi

Servings: 2-3

Ingredients:

1 cup mango juice

½ cup coconut water

1 cup pineapple juice

2 tablespoons sugar

Preparation:

1. Combine mango juice, coconut water, pineapple juice, and sugar in a large pitcher and whisk until the sugar is fully dissolved.
2. Pour the mixture into the Ninja Slushi vessel.
3. Select "FROZEN JUICE." The preset will start at the default/optimal temperature, which is excellent for the best texture.
4. If you'd like, you can modify the temperature to your preference.
5. When the frozen drink attains the desired temperature, the machine will beep three times.
6. Dispense and enjoy.

Apple Kiwi Frozen Juice Slushi

Servings: 4

Ingredients:

2 cups apple juice

2 cups kiwi juice

2 to 3 tablespoons sugar

Preparation:

1. Combine all ingredients in a large pitcher and whisk until the sugar is fully dissolved.

2. Pour the mixture into the Ninja Slushi vessel.

3. Select "FROZEN JUICE." The preset will start at the default/optimal temperature, which is excellent for the best texture.

4. If you'd like, you can modify the temperature to your preference.

5. When the frozen drink attains the desired temperature, the machine will beep three times.

6. Dispense and enjoy.

Apple and Cranberry Frozen Juice Slushi

Servings: 4

Ingredients:

2 cups cranberry juice

2 cups apple juice, fresh or store-bought

2 tablespoons sugar

Preparation:

1. Combine cranberry juice, apple juice, and sugar in a large pitcher and whisk until the sugar is fully dissolved.

2. Pour the mixture into the Ninja Slushi vessel.

3. Select "FROZEN JUICE." The preset will start at the default/optimal temperature, which is excellent for the best texture.

4. If you'd like, you can modify the temperature to your preference.

5. When the frozen drink attains the desired temperature, the machine will beep three times.

6. Dispense and enjoy.

Lime Cherry Frozen Juice Slushi

Servings: 4

Ingredients:

2 cups cherry juice (or fresh cherries blended into juice)

2 tablespoons sugar

1 cup fresh lime juice

Preparation:

1. Combine all ingredients in a large pitcher and whisk until the sugar is fully dissolved.
2. Pour the mixture into the Ninja Slushi vessel.
3. Select "FROZEN JUICE." The preset will start at the default/optimal temperature, which is excellent for the best texture.
4. If you'd like, you can modify the temperature to your preference.
5. When the frozen drink attains the desired temperature, the machine will beep three times.
6. Dispense and enjoy.

Pineapple and Passionfruit Frozen Juice Slushi

Servings: 4

Ingredients:

2 cups passionfruit juice

2 cups pineapple juice

2 to 3 tablespoons sugar

Preparation:

1. Combine passionfruit juice, pineapple juice, and sugar in a large pitcher and whisk until the sugar is fully dissolved.
2. Pour the mixture into the Ninja Slushi vessel.
3. Select "FROZEN JUICE." The preset will start at the default/optimal temperature, which is excellent for the best texture.
4. If you'd like, you can modify the temperature to your preference.
5. When the frozen drink attains the desired temperature, the machine will beep three times.
6. Dispense and enjoy.

Orange-Raspberry Frozen Juice Slushi

Servings: 4

Ingredients:

2 cups orange juice

2 to 3 tablespoons sugar

2 raspberries juice

Preparation:

1. Combine all ingredients in a large pitcher and whisk until the sugar is fully dissolved.
2. Pour the mixture into the Ninja Slushi vessel.
3. Select "FROZEN JUICE." The preset will start at the default/optimal temperature, which is excellent for the best texture.
4. If you'd like, you can modify the temperature to your preference.
5. When the frozen drink attains the desired temperature, the machine will beep three times.
6. Dispense and enjoy.

Coconut Pineapple Frozen Juice Slushi

Servings: 4

Ingredients:

2 cups pineapple juice

2 cups coconut water

¼ cup fresh lime juice

1 cup cold coconut cream

¼ cup of sugar

Preparation:

1. Combine all ingredients in a large pitcher and whisk until the sugar is fully dissolved.
2. Pour the mixture into the Ninja Slushi vessel.
3. Select "FROZEN JUICE." The preset will start at the default/optimal temperature, which is excellent for the best texture.
4. If you'd like, you can modify the temperature to your preference.
5. When the frozen drink attains the desired temperature, the machine will beep three times.
6. Dispense and enjoy.

Coconut Watermelon Frozen Juice Slushi

Servings: 4

Ingredients:

2 cups watermelon juice

2 to 3 tablespoons sugar

2 cups coconut water

1 tablespoon lime juice

Preparation:

1.Combine watermelon juice, coconut water, lime juice, and sugar in a large pitcher and whisk until the sugar is fully dissolved.

2.Pour the mixture into the Ninja Slushi vessel.

3.Select "FROZEN JUICE." The preset will start at the default/optimal temperature, which is excellent for the best texture.

4.If you'd like, you can modify the temperature to your preference.

5.When the frozen drink attains the desired temperature, the machine will beep three times.

6.Dispense and enjoy.

Blueberry Pomegranate Frozen Juice Slushi

Servings: 4

Ingredients:

2 cups pomegranate juice

2 to 3 tablespoons sugar

2 cups blueberry juice

Preparation:

1.Combine all ingredients in a large pitcher and whisk until the sugar is fully dissolved.

2.Pour the mixture into the Ninja Slushi vessel.

3.Select "FROZEN JUICE." The preset will start at the default/optimal temperature, which is excellent for the best texture.

4.If you'd like, you can modify the temperature to your preference.

5.When the frozen drink attains the desired temperature, the machine will beep three times.

6.Dispense and enjoy.

Flavorful Passion Fruit Frozen Juice Slushi

Servings: 2

Ingredients:

2 cups passion fruit juice   2 tablespoons sugar

Preparation:

1. Put the juice and sugar into a large-sized pitcher and whisk to dissolve the sugar.
2. Pour the mixture into the Ninja Slushi vessel.
3. Select "FROZEN JUICE." The preset will start at the default/optimal temperature, which is excellent for the best texture.
4. If you prefer, you can adjust the temperature.
5. When the frozen drink attains the desired temperature, the machine will beep three times.
6. Serve immediately and enjoy.

Easy Black Grapes Frozen Juice Slushi

Servings: 2

Ingredients:

2 cups black grapes juice   2 tablespoons sugar

Preparation:

1. Put the juice and sugar into a large-sized pitcher and whisk to dissolve the sugar.
2. Pour the mixture into the Ninja Slushi vessel.
3. Select "FROZEN JUICE." The preset will start at the default/optimal temperature, which is excellent for the best texture.
4. If you prefer, you can adjust the temperature.
5. When the frozen drink attains the desired temperature, the machine will beep three times.
6. Serve immediately and enjoy.

Banana Strawberry Frozen Juice Slushi

Servings: 2

**Ingredients:**

2 cups bottled banana strawberry smoothie   2 tablespoons sugar

Preparation:

1.Put the smoothie and sugar into a large pitcher and whisk to dissolve the sugar.

2.Pour the mixture into the Ninja Slushi vessel.

3.Select "FROZEN JUICE." The preset will start at the default/optimal temperature, which is excellent for the best texture.

4.If you prefer, you can adjust the temperature.

5.When the frozen drink attains the desired temperature, the machine will beep three times.

6.Serve immediately and enjoy.

Cherry Frozen Juice Slushi

Servings: 2

Ingredients:

2 cups cherry juice   2 tablespoons sugar

Preparation:

1.Put the juice and sugar into a large-sized pitcher and whisk to dissolve the sugar.

2.Pour the mixture into the Ninja Slushi vessel.

3.Select "FROZEN JUICE." The preset will start at the default/optimal temperature, which is excellent for the best texture.

4.If you prefer, you can adjust the temperature.

5.When the frozen drink attains the desired temperature, the machine will beep three times.

6.Serve immediately and enjoy.

Orange Pineapple Frozen Juice Slushi

Servings: 2

Ingredients:

1 cup pineapple juice

1 cup orange juice

2 tablespoons sugar

Preparation:

1. Put the juices and sugar into a large-sized pitcher and whisk to dissolve the sugar.

2. Pour the mixture into the Ninja Slushi vessel.

3. Select "FROZEN JUICE." The preset will start at the default/optimal temperature, which is excellent for the best texture.

4. If you prefer, you can adjust the temperature.

5. When the frozen drink attains the desired temperature, the machine will beep three times.

6. Serve immediately and enjoy.

Mango Peach Frozen Juice Slushi

Servings: 2

Ingredients:

2 cups bottled mango peach smoothie

2 tablespoons sugar

Preparation:

1. Put the smoothie and sugar into a large pitcher and whisk to dissolve the sugar.

2. Pour the mixture into the Ninja Slushi vessel.

3. Select "FROZEN JUICE." The preset will start at the default/optimal temperature, which is excellent for the best texture.

4. If you prefer, you can adjust the temperature.

5. When the frozen drink attains the desired temperature, the machine will beep three times.

6. Serve immediately and enjoy.

Simple Orange Frozen Juice Slushi

Servings: 2

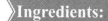 **Ingredients:**

2 cups orange juice   2 tablespoons sugar

Preparation:

1.Put the juice and sugar into a large-sized pitcher and whisk to dissolve the sugar.

2.Pour the mixture into the Ninja Slushi vessel.

3.Select "FROZEN JUICE." The preset will start at the default/optimal temperature, which is excellent for the best texture.

4.If you prefer, you can adjust the temperature.

5.When the frozen drink attains the desired temperature, the machine will beep three times.

6.Serve immediately and enjoy.

Tropical Fruits Coconut Frozen Juice Slushi

Servings: 2-3

Ingredients:

1 cup pineapple juice   ½ cup coconut water
½ cup mango juice   2 tablespoons sugar
1 cup orange juice

Preparation:

1.Put the juices, coconut water, and sugar into a large-sized pitcher and whisk to dissolve the sugar.

2.Pour the mixture into the Ninja Slushi vessel.

3.Select "FROZEN JUICE." The preset will start at the default/optimal temperature, which is excellent for the best texture.

4.If you prefer, you can adjust the temperature.

5.When the frozen drink attains the desired temperature, the machine will beep three times.

6.Serve immediately and enjoy.

Conclusion

The Ninja Slushi Professional Frozen Drink Maker and its companion Ninja Slushi Recipe Book are the ultimate tools to transform your beverage-making experience. Whether you're crafting icy treats for a summer gathering, experimenting with new flavors for a weekend indulgence, or preparing a healthier frozen alternative for your family, these tools make it effortless to achieve perfection every time.

With the Ninja Slushi, you can create an incredible variety of drinks, from classic slushies and creamy milkshakes to elegant frappés and vibrant frozen juices. Its RapidChill Technology and intuitive presets ensure consistently smooth textures and perfectly chilled results, catering to both casual enthusiasts and culinary adventurers. The dual focus on convenience and innovation means you can enjoy high-quality drinks without the hassle of complicated processes or lengthy preparation times.

The Ninja Slushi Recipe Book complements the machine perfectly, offering a wide array of recipes that inspire creativity and cater to various tastes. From tropical fruit combinations to indulgent dessert-style drinks, every recipe is designed to maximize the potential of your Ninja Slushi.

Investing in the Ninja Slushi and its recipe book means embracing versatility, ease of use, and endless possibilities in frozen drink-making. These tools empower you to elevate everyday moments, impress guests with delightful creations, and indulge in your personal favorites—all with the push of a button.

Don't wait—unlock the joy of professional-quality frozen drinks at home today! Whether you're hosting a party or unwinding after a long day, the Ninja Slushi Professional Frozen Drink Maker and Recipe Book will help you savor every sip.

Appendix 1 Measurement Conversion Chart

VOLUME EQUIVALENTS (LIQUID)

US STANDARD	US STANDARD (OUNCES)	METRIC (APPROXIMATE)
2 tablespoons	1 fl.oz	30 mL
¼ cup	2 fl.oz	60 mL
½ cup	4 fl.oz	120 mL
1 cup	8 fl.oz	240 mL
1½ cup	12 fl.oz	355 mL
2 cups or 1 pint	16 fl.oz	475 mL
4 cups or 1 quart	32 fl.oz	1 L
1 gallon	128 fl.oz	4 L

VOLUME EQUIVALENTS (DRY)

US STANDARD	METRIC (APPROXIMATE)
⅛ teaspoon	0.5 mL
¼ teaspoon	1 mL
½ teaspoon	2 mL
¾ teaspoon	4 mL
1 teaspoon	5 mL
1 tablespoon	15 mL
¼ cup	59 mL
½ cup	118 mL
¾ cup	177 mL
1 cup	235 mL
2 cups	475 mL
3 cups	700 mL
4 cups	1 L

TEMPERATURES EQUIVALENTS

FAHRENHEIT(F)	CELSIUS（C) (APPROXIMATE)
225 °F	107 °C
250 °F	120 °C
275 °F	135 °C
300 °F	150 °C
325 °F	160 °C
350 °F	180 °C
375 °F	190 °C
400 °F	205 °C
425 °F	220 °C
450 °F	235 °C
475 °F	245 °C
500 °F	260 °C

WEIGHT EQUIVALENTS

US STANDARD	METRIC (APPROXINATE)
1 ounce	28 g
2 ounces	57 g
5 ounces	142 g
10 ounces	284 g
15 ounces	425 g
16 ounces (1 pound)	455 g
1.5pounds	680 g
2pounds	907 g

Appendix 2 Recipes Index

A

Almond Chocolate Milkshake Slushi 80

Apple and Cranberry Frozen Juice Slushi 87

Apple Kiwi Frozen Juice Slushi 87

Aromatic Martini Slushi 42

Banana Chocolate Chip Vanilla Milkshake Slushi 71

B

Banana Date Milkshake Slushi 74

Banana Oats Milkshake Slushi 75

Banana Strawberry Frozen Juice Slushi 92

Basic Mango Slushi 26

Berries Banana Slushi 26

Blueberry Frappé Slushi 69

Blueberry Pomegranate Frozen Juice Slushi 90

C

Caramel Pretzel Milkshake Slushi 80

Caramel Tiramisu Frappé Slushi 67

Carrot Tangerine Frozen Juice Slushi 86

Cherry Frozen Juice Slushi 92

Cherry Pomegranate Slushi 22

Chocolate Cookie-Kahlua Milkshake Slushi 72

Chocolate Frappé Slushi 64

Chocolate Peanut Butter Milkshake Slushi 79

Cinnamon Apple Shake Slushi 72

Cinnamon Chocolate Slushi 18

Cinnamon Hazelnut Frappé Slushi 63

Cinnamon Peach Milkshake Slushi 83

Citrus White Wine Slushi 40

Classic Bloody Mary Slushi 42

Classic Margarita Slushi 36

Classic Peach Bellini Slushi 48

Cocoa Frappe Slushi 60

Coconut Pineapple Frozen Juice Slushi 89

Coconut Pineapple Milkshake Slushi 82

Coconut Pineapple Slushi 16

Coconut Pineapple Slushi 20

Coconut Watermelon Frozen Juice Slushi 90

Cream Cheese Milkshake Slushi 77

Creamy Banana Nutella Milkshake Slushi 79

Creamy Mango Frappe Slushi 60

Cucumber & Honeydew Melon Slushi 18

D

Delicious Mango Frappé Slushi 66

Delicious Mudslide Slushi 46

Delicious Pomegranate Gin Slushi 41

E

Easy Black Grapes Frozen Juice Slushi 91

Easy Butterscotch Milkshake Slushi 78

Espresso Chocolate Frappe Slushi 57

F

Flavorful Margarita Cocktail Slushi 46

Flavorful Matcha Tea Slushi 32

Flavorful Passion Fruit Frozen Juice Slushi 91

Flavorful Pineapple Orange Slushi 23

Flavorful Vanilla Frappe Slushi 56

Fresh Grape Lemonade Slushi 27

Fresh Raspberry Lemonade Slushi 28

Fresh Strawberry Frappe Slushi 61

G

Ginger Peach Slushi 31

Ginger Pineapple Slushi 29

Grape and Blueberry Slushi 23

Green Tea Frappe Slushi 64

H

Homemade Caramel Frappe Slushi 62

Homemade Champagne Cocktail Slushi 35

Homemade Chocolate Hazelnut Milkshake Slushi 84

Homemade Citrus Blend Slushi 21

Honeydew Rum Slushi 37

K

KitKat Vanilla Milkshake Slushi 77

L

Lemon Cucumber Gin Slushi 51

Lemon Lime Sprite Slushi 32

Lemon Strawberry Daiquiri Slushi 45

Lemon Strawberry Vodka Slushi 39

Lemonade Cherry Slushi 17

Lemonade Spiked Slushi 49

Lime Cherry Frozen Juice Slushi 88

Lime Cranberry Vodka Slushi 52

Lime Cucumber Slushi 33

Lime Gin and Tonic Slushi 53
Lime Grapefruit Paloma Slushi 47
Lime Margaritas Slushi 38
Lime Watermelon Slushi 25
Lime Yogurt Frappe Slushi 57

M
Mango Cantaloupe Slushi 22
Mango Peach Frozen Juice Slushi 93
Mango Slushi 31
Matcha Frappe Slushi 58
Mint Blackberry Bourbon Slushi 47
Mint Chocolate Chip Vanilla Milkshake Slushi 75
Mint Chocolate Milkshake Slushi 83
Mint Honeydew Slushi 19
Mint Orange Slushi 27
Mint Watermelon Tequila Slushi 50
Minty Berries Slushi 20
Mixed Berries Slushi 16
Moscato Pomegranate Slushi 36

O
Orange Pineapple Frozen Juice Slushi 93
Orange Tequila Slushi 44
Orange Vanilla Milkshake Slushi 82
Orange-Raspberry Frozen Juice Slushi 89
Oreo and Cream Frappe Slushi 59
Oreo Vanilla Milkshake Slushi 81

P
Paloma Spiked Slushi 41
Passion Fruit Cocktail Slushi 53
Passion Fruit Rum Slushi 39
Peach and Basil Slushi 17
Peach Mango Slushi 24
Peach Tea Slushi 33
Peanut Butter Vanilla Milkshake Slushi 71
Pineapple and Passionfruit Frozen Juice Slushi 88
Pineapple Colada Slushi 52
Pineapple Milkshake Slushi 73
Pineapple Rum Slushi 35
Pumpkin Frappe Slushi 61
Pumpkin Milkshake Slushi 81

R
Raspberry and Cookies Frappe Slushi 62
Raspberry Peach Slushi 43

Raspberry Slushi 28
Raspberry White Chocolate Frappé Slushi 67
Refreshing Blue Lagoon Slushi 49
Refreshing Mojito Slushi 43
Refreshing Peach, Apricot, and Orange Slushi 19
Refreshing Watermelon Strawberry Slushi 30
Rich Grape Slushi 25

S
Salted Caramel Vanilla Milkshake Slushi 74
Sangria Red Wine Slushi 45
Simple Brownie Milkshake Slushi 73
Simple Coconut Frappé Slushi 69
Simple Orange Frozen Juice Slushi 94
Smooth Double Chocolate Frappé Slushi 65
Sparkling Berries Slushi 44
Sparkling Peach White Wine Slushi 54
Spiked Pina Rum Slushi 40
Strawberry Frappe Slushi 58
Strawberry Kiwi Slushi 24
Strawberry Rum Slushi 37
Sweet Lemonade Slushi 38

T
Tasty Cherry Cola Slushi 21
Tasty Mai Tai Slushi 50
The Best Tiramisu Frappe Slushi 59
Tropical Fruits Coconut Frozen Juice Slushi 94
Tropical Mango Pineapple Frozen Juice Slushi 86
Tropical Rum Slushi 51
Tropical Twist Slushi 29

V
Vanilla Blueberry Milkshake Slushi 76
Vanilla Chocolate Frappe Slushi 56
Vanilla Eggnog Bourbon Slushi 48
Vanilla Frappé Slushi 63
Vanilla Matcha Green Tea Frappé Slushi 66
Vanilla Milkshake Slushi 78
Vanilla Root Beer Slushi 30
Vanilla Strawberry Frappé Slushi 65

W
Walnut Milkshake Slushi 76
Walnut Oatmeal Frappé Slushi 68
Whiskey Frappé Slushi 68

Made in United States
Orlando, FL
17 December 2024

56043666R00062